Free from Dogma

Tom Raits

5th April 2009

Tom Ravetz

Free from Dogma

Theological Reflections
in The Christian Community

Floris Books

First published in 2009 by Floris Books

© 2009 Tom Ravetz
The author has asserted his right under the
Copyright, Design and Patents Act 1988
to be identified as the Author of this Work.

British Library CIP Data available

ISBN 978-086315-690-8

Printed in Great Britain
by Bell & Bain, Glasgow

Contents

To Deborah, my inspiration, and to Christiaan,
in gratitude to the most devoted collaborator.

Prologue:

The Journey from Unity to Community

The beginning is one — single — a unity. Everything is infolded. The whole multitude of things — animals and atoms, stars and galaxies, all the experiences and thoughts of human beings and angels — exist as pure potential within God. Time is not yet. Space is infolded. Then God's fullness overflows in a free deed of pure, creative love.

The world around us with all its abundance, its fullness and variety of separate, individual things — it all springs forth from this ground. Stones and plants; animals, human beings, angels and other heavenly powers — all pour forth from him in over-flowing generosity. Science tells the story of the simplest atoms that condensed to become the elements, nebulae, stars; that seeded galaxies. All the glory of the night sky issues forth from this vast outpouring of energy. And that is only a story about the outside of what happens. The inside is pure, self-bestowing love.

Every human soul, every feeling, every breath — all of it is inside God as potential before it pours out into existence. Unimaginable variety comes from this single origin. So great is God's love that it allows what has been created to stretch so far from God that it becomes other than God. World exists over against God, separate from God, even opposed to God — *and the light shines in the darkness, and the darkness has not grasped it.* Ranks of spiritual beings — God's hands and feet, his limbs, eyes and ears — work on the world, shining down their thoughts, drawing the world to evolve towards higher perfection.

A creature made in God's image walks on the earth, a creator in becoming, bearing the seed of God's word, godlike already in naming and understanding, in finding and giving meaning.

In the beginning human beings worship the multitude of spiritual beings that they experience within and behind all that is — the hands and feet, eyes and ears of God. The ancient Jewish people are the forerunners with the hard task of understanding that there is one central being at the heart of everything; one unifying principle that underlies all of creation with all its manifold details and glories. The worship of this God allows human beings to become unitary beings themselves. *I believe in one God — one almighty divine being.*

With the coming of Christ and the sending of the Holy Spirit, God reveals himself as one in three and three in one. At Whitsun, many tongues of flame emerge from the one central flame. Each individual human being can become a bearer of Holy Spirit. The splitting and splintering of humanity that started at the Tower of Babel, symbol of human beings' growing separation on their journey, is overcome. At Whitsun, the apostles' words resonate in the souls of those who hear them, regardless of whether they understand them with their minds. The very beings of those who hear them vibrate in unison as the words recall their common origin in the spirit.

A new unity is born — not a simple oneness, but community, the place of common life, of common work and striving. This is *ekklesia*, the assembly of those called out to perform a service for the world. They overcome the great divisions that splinter humanity — *in Christ there is neither Jew nor Greek, man nor woman, slave nor free,* says Saint Paul (Galatians 3:28). In their celebration they rejoice in a new joining of heaven and earth, a foreshadowing of the fulfilment when God will be 'all in all' (1 Corinthians 15:28). They celebrate their vocation as human beings: to join together in a new community with creation — with all human beings — with the divine world.

This human community is neither uniform nor exclusive. It is not regimented, 'churchy' in any old sense. It celebrates all creativity that is in tune with the abundance of the life and love which is the ultimate reality. It seeks for the truth about the journey that we are on, not to prescribe a dogma but to help human beings on their journey. At the heart of the community is celebration and rejoicing. When the prodigal son of the parable returns, the father rejoices. This my son, he says, was lost and is found. He was dead and has come back to life. When human beings find their true vocation in the celebration of community they find themselves again, and pass from death to life.

Introduction:

Did Not Our Hearts Burn Within Us?

That very day two of them were going to a village
named Emmaus, about seven miles from Jerusalem, and
talking with each other about all these things that had
happened. While they were talking and discussing
together, Jesus himself drew near and went with them.
But their eyes were kept from recognizing him. And he
said to them, 'What is this conversation which you are
holding with each other as you walk?' And they stood
still, looking sad. Then one of them, named Cleopas,
answered him, 'Are you the only visitor to Jerusalem
who does not know the things that have happened there
in these days?' And he said to them, 'What things?' And
they said to him, 'Concerning Jesus of Nazareth, who
was a prophet mighty in deed and word before God and
all the people, and how our chief priests and rulers deliv-
ered him up to be condemned to death, and crucified
him. But we had hoped that he was the one to redeem
Israel. ... And he said to them, 'O foolish men, and slow
of heart to believe all that the prophets have spoken! Was
it not necessary that the Christ should suffer these things
and enter into his glory?' And beginning with Moses and
all the prophets, he interpreted to them in all the scriptures the things concerning himself. So they drew near to
the village to which they were going. He appeared to be
going further, but they constrained him, saying, 'Stay
with us, for it is toward evening and the day is now far
spent.' So he went in to stay with them. When he was at

table with them, he took the bread and blessed, and
broke it, and gave it to them. And their eyes were opened
and they recognized him; and he vanished out of their
sight. They said to each other, 'Did not our hearts burn
within us while he talked to us on the road, while he
opened to us the scriptures?'
(Luke 24:13–32, RSV)

On the first Easter Sunday, the disciples grieved the bitter loss,
not only of their beloved master, but also of their hopes and
expectations. Even now, after two thousand years have passed,
we struggle to understand that the saviour of Israel and all of
humankind has to pass through suffering in order to be revealed
in his glory. For the disciples it seemed quite impossible that
good could come from the tragedy that they had experienced.
Christ does not comfort them with empty reassurances that
their hope will be fulfilled as they imagined it. He tells them
about the Hebrew Scriptures, which they, as Jews, knew well.
Now that the hard shell of their assumptions has been cracked
open by their grief, they can hear a new way of understanding
the familiar texts. In their grieving hearts, a purifying fire is
kindled. This fire prepares them to experience the glory of the
risen Christ in a way that they had never expected, not at the
head of an avenging army of national liberation, but as sharer of
the broken bread — symbol of his broken body — at the supper
table, who invites them into communion with himself.

This is the birth of Christian theology.

A thousand years later, Anselm of Canterbury said that theology was 'faith seeking understanding.' Faith for him meant
something that we experience. In the story of Emmaus, theology
gives the disciples the key to understand their experience of loss
and grief. It prepares them for an experience of fulfilment and
community. From the beginning theology was part of the
process of the purification of the heart, making it into an organ
of perception for the glory of God, which appears in ways we
never really learn to expect.

The first use of theology was *catechesis* — the instruction of
new members. In the early church, those who were to be baptized, who were not yet permitted to attend the mystery of the

Eucharist, underwent an intensive preparation during Passiontide. They learnt to see their lives up to this moment in the light of the Gospel. They saw that what they had cherished and made most important, was vain. They recognized that these most cherished things become our God, and that they were worshipping not the Ground of all Being, but the idols of honour, possessions and success. They spent the night of Holy Saturday in a vigil, after which they undressed. Cyril, Bishop of Jerusalem in the fourth century, taught those newly baptized how to understand what happened to them in this state:

> undressing was an image of putting off the old man with his deeds. Having stripped yourselves, ye were naked ... For since the adverse powers made their lair in your members, ye may no longer wear that old garment ... O wondrous thing! you were naked in the sight of all, and were not ashamed; for truly you bore the likeness of the first-formed Adam, who was naked in the garden, and was not ashamed.
> *(Mystagogical Catechism* II)

Jacques Lusseyran, the blind fighter in the French Resistance, describes how some of the people who were selected for work in the concentration camps were immediately crushed by the experience of being stripped and shaved. They could not withstand the loss of their outer persona, the way they saw themselves and wanted others to see them. For others it was the beginning of a new life, even in the terrible circumstances of the camps.

After stripping and being exorcized, the candidates were led into the church or baptistery. Three times they were immersed in the baptismal water; three times they were asked 'Do you believe...' — first in the Father, then in the Son, then in the Holy Spirit. They had to answer each time, as they were being drawn out of the water: 'Credo!' — 'I believe!' They knew through their preparation that in entering and leaving the water, they were passing from death to life. Saint Paul never tires of teaching his congregations this:

> We were buried therefore with him by baptism into
> death, so that as Christ was raised from the dead by the
> glory of the Father, we too might walk in newness of life.
> For if we have been united with him in a death like his,
> we shall certainly be united with him in a resurrection
> like his.
>
> We know that our old self was crucified with him so
> that the sinful body might be destroyed, and we might
> no longer be enslaved to sin. ... But if we have died with
> Christ, we believe that we shall also live with him. For
> we know that Christ being raised from the dead will
> never die again; death no longer has dominion over him.
> (Romans 5:5–9, RSV)

Cyril reminds his hearers of their experience in his church in
Jerusalem, where the candidates could look at the shrine of the
Holy Sepulchre:

> After these things, ye were led to the holy pool of Divine
> Baptism, as Christ was carried from the Cross to the
> Sepulchre which is before our eyes. And each of you was
> asked, whether he believed in the name of the Father, and
> of the Son, and of the Holy Spirit, and ye made that saving
> confession, and descended three times into the water, and
> ascended again; here also hinting by a symbol at the three
> days' burial of Christ. ... And at the self-same moment ye
> were both dying and being born; and that water of salva-
> tion was at once your grave and your mother. ...
>
> O strange and inconceivable thing! We did not really
> die, we were not really buried, we were not really cruci-
> fied and raised again; but our imitation was in a figure,
> and our salvation in reality. Christ was actually crucified,
> and actually buried, and truly rose again; and all these
> things He has freely bestowed upon us, that we, sharing
> His sufferings by imitation, might gain salvation in reality.
> *(Mystagogical Catechism* II)

The candidates went through a kind of emptying of the heart in
the experience of dying with Christ. Out of their experience of

their old self dying, they were prepared to participate in the Eucharist, the gift of the one who broke bread in their midst. A final step came afterwards, probably the following year, when Cyril's sermons gave them the concepts to understand what they had experienced so powerfully the year before.

In Passiontide we experience an echo of these powerful experiences. In The Christian Community, the Epistle (the seasonal prayer at the beginning of the Act of Consecration of Man) speaks of the heart being empty, and of the experience of loss. The Creed (from Latin *credo* — I believe) reminds us of the fundamental truths of creation — redemption — consecration. Then we are ready to experience the glory, the re-appearance of the one who died and was reborn, who joins us at the table and whose presence we know, as the disciples did in Emmaus, through his breaking and sharing bread, giving and sharing himself. What experiences of emptiness and loss do we go through before we arrive in the Act of Consecration of Man? Life itself can provide them. Beyond this, Sacramental Consultation offers a way of preparing consciously for the communion with the one who appears at the table, breaking bread and giving himself.

Theology in becoming

Theology existed before Christ. Theology is a Greek word, made up of two other words: *Theos*, meaning God, and *logos*, meaning word, thought, meaning, study, law. The simplest translation of theology would be 'words about God' — some theologians today like to speak of 'God-talk.' But *logos* has a much wider meaning than this. We meet it in words like geology and biology — the study of the earth and of life. For the ancient Greeks, the word about something meant much more than just a collection of facts about a subject. They never forgot that *logos* or word is the faculty that raises human beings from the level of the animal world, their link with the divine 'poet,' whose words lie at the root of all creation. The *logos* of a thing is its essence, the thought that existed in the mind of God when he created it. So 'theology' is thinking about God and the Divine in the widest sense

— thinking that participates in God's very essence. Unlike all the other '-logies,' in theology the divine power of thinking reflects upon its own source. Subject and object become one when logos-power reflects on the nature of the *Logos* itself.

Theology in ancient Greece was the study of the myths about the gods. The Greek philosophers, who celebrated the birth of the liberating power of human thinking that needed no myths, despised theologians. In Christianity, theology took on a new role. Early Christians had access to a world of powerful new experiences. From the start, they longed to understand what they experienced. As we saw above, Jesus Christ was the first to teach Christian theology, interpreting the Hebrew Scriptures to give the disciples concepts to understand their experience of himself.

There is no real parallel in the history of other religions to the theological ferment and controversies of the first five centuries of Christianity. In fact, the concept of theology seems to have been alien to the other world religions until contact with Christianity made them formulate their own theologies. This ferment is often seen as a negative aspect of the life of the church; it certainly led to agony and even bloodshed. Once the Roman Emperors were involved, theological discussion became mixed up with politics, and the manoeuvrings that accompanied the Church Councils make unappetizing reading. However, the preoccupation with theology reflects something deeper. It marks a new step in human development. In ancient times, when they were closer to the original unity with God, human beings received inspiration directly from spiritual beings. Their journey takes them from the status of receiver of truth to that of co-creator of truth. In the Epistle that is read at the beginning of the Act of Consecration of Man between festival times, our thoughts are directed to the Trinity. The first two paragraphs contain statements about the being of God the Father and the world's becoming through the creative Word. The third paragraph does not contain statements but exhortations, prayers. There are no statements to make about God the Holy Spirit. We can only pray for a mutual interpenetration: that his light should shine in our knowing; that he should receive our knowing into his life. The life of the Trinity finds its completion in our thinking.

In the earliest centuries theology could still call on powers which had been there in abundance in the religious cultures of antiquity. Origen (185–253), one of the greatest teachers of the early church, teaches partly through reason and argument, partly by recalling myths. These resound in the souls of his pupils and fill out what they have experienced themselves. Gradually as the centuries go by, theology becomes less a support for experience than a substitute for it. There are more and more arguments amongst theologians. Then dogmas start to be defined. A living world of experience is gradually distilled into fixed forms. This goes hand in hand with the rooting out of 'paganism.' Human beings were not permitted to experience the divine outside of themselves in the glories of nature. They were thrown back on themselves. They repeated what the Jewish people had achieved in Old Testament times: the lonely journey towards a unitary selfhood.

This long process of abstraction reached a climax in the nineteenth century. The Enlightenment was the final liberation of human reason from every shackle of dogma and revealed truth. Reason beat down every door that stood in its way. First the Old Testament and then the New were subjected to critical examination. Humanity liberated itself from half-understood dogmas from the past. But this liberation brought with it a bitter loss. Any idea that dogmas had their origin in spiritual experience was lost. Theology threatened to reduce Jesus to a teacher of simple moral rules. When Friedrich Nietzsche (1844–1900) reported the statement that God is dead, this was true in a way. The dogmatically formulated doctrine of the Trinity was dead — it was an empty shell. Friedrich Schleiermacher (1768–1834), the father of modern theology, sought the way back to a living theology of experience. Rejecting dogma, he fell back on the description of something quite general — the 'God-consciousness,' the 'feeling of absolute dependency.' Jesus is called Son of God because in him this consciousness was alive to an unprecedented degree. He is the greatest human being who embodies what all must strive for. Perhaps symbolically, Schleiermacher relegated the Trinity to the last chapter of his book, *The Christian Faith*. The theology of experience becomes mere subjectivity. There is little defence before the accusation of

Ludwig Feuerbach (1804–72) and Karl Marx (1818–83) that God is nothing but a projection of human qualities, hopes and aspirations on to an imaginary super-being.

The modern world

The situation of the religious soul at the beginning of the twentieth century was something like that of the disciples on the road to Emmaus. An old picture of God and old hopes of redemption were lost. In the fundamentalist movements, we see a reaction to the pain this caused. Using literal methods of interpretation which would have puzzled previous generations, fundamentalists try to shore up some certainty in a world that seems to have lost its direction. Others turn away from spirituality altogether, and seek meaning in a world without spirit.

Fundamentalists reject the human power of thinking, placing authority in revealed texts. But we have seen above that theology — the logos-power used to understand the *Logos* itself — is a fulfilment of creation. Are we really to believe that this was all a mistake; that the great advances human beings have made through their thinking were a cul-de-sac?

Neither fundamentalism nor scepticism gives an answer that goes *through* the experience of loss and transcends it, as the disciples were able to do in Emmaus. In the heart of the Act of Consecration of Man, where Jesus Christ appears at the altar-table, breaking bread and sharing wine, there is a revolutionary new rendering of his words. Where in the old liturgies, based on the gospel texts, we hear 'do this in remembrance of me,' now we hear a charge to 'take this into your thinking.' The path we saw at the beginning is repeated: we come from the world which has lost its comfort; we encounter the living Lord; now we need to *think* about what has happened. It goes further when we hear that Christ's death, resurrection and glorification will 'think in us.'

But the sacraments do not instantly transfer us into a new state of being; they inaugurate processes. As in the early church, Passiontide is the time when the process of becoming followers of Christ begins. However long we may have known him, we need to become beginners again and again. The prayer speaks to the empty heart of the human being and reminds us of our loss; in the Holy Week our heart starts to burn. Only on Easter Sunday is the heart filled with new life.

There is another step. In the Easter prayer we hear that Christ has arisen as 'the meaning of the earth.' We hear too a command: our word should sound forth, awakened by the Spirit. The knowledge of the earth's meaning — that is to say, the knowledge that it 'was necessary that the Christ should suffer these things and enter into his glory' — is not our private possession. We are ourselves on the road to Emmaus, grieving our losses, and we know many others on this road. We are called to find words that will reach our fellow human beings in their grief — words that will kindle the flame of their hearts. This is not just the job of priests; the whole church has a priestly task of witness to the world. And we know all too well that repeating dogmatic statements does not meet human beings in their need. It is not a question of saying certain churchy words, but opening ourselves to others and showing that we too know the pain of loss and uncertainty.

Only when the church became an instrument of Roman state policy in the fourth century did it become important to establish and enforce norms of belief. Today there is a need to find once more the spirit of free celebration that was there in the beginnings of the church. Human beings need to celebrate the reality of Christ as he approaches us today, without submitting to dogma. The Christian Community strives to make this possible.

Along with this central activity of celebrating, human souls need to understand what they experience in community — the sacraments and the Gospels. There is a more reflective, intellectual task to be fulfilled here, which has been of equal importance in The Christian Community since its foundation in 1922. It has found help in the reflections of twenty centuries in which Christians have grappled to understand their experiences. Even the driest of dogmas can provide a kind of grammar, a framework within which a living theology can develop.

There is another source for thinking about these experiences, one neglected by most theologians of the modern era: that is the work of Rudolf Steiner (1861–1925). His works do not provide the answer to every question; but again and again his insights show a way forward that transcends the seeming impasse between dogmatically received truth and the critical spirit of modern thinking. They can lead on from experiences that we already have, giving them a wider context. This book is not peppered with quotations from Steiner because it is not intended to be a presentation of Steiner's work. Nevertheless, the whole book would not have been possible without the framework he provides. A key element of this is his conception of the evolution of consciousness — the idea that human beings are on a journey from an original unity with the spirit towards selfhood.[1] The consequence of this journey and the urgent need for the Incarnation of Christ as a counterbalancing tendency is the theme of countless lecture cycles.[2] The concept of the evolution of consciousness makes it possible to look at ideas and ritual practices as they have evolved, seeing in them the fruits of their respective epoch of human development. In the central issue of Christology, it can be shown how the classical theological tradition can often take us to the point of an abstract schema. The insights that Rudolf Steiner provides can fill such a schema with life.

Even more important, if less sensational than the results of his own researches, is Steiner's description of a path of self-development which can awaken organs that perceive the spirit as vividly and as clearly as our sense organs see the phenomenal world. This is described in a classic way in his book, *Knowledge of the Higher Worlds — How is it Achieved?* This book also makes it clear that long before one has advanced to the level of perception that Steiner attained, the method of inner schooling can give one confidence in the results of one's own thinking.

* * *

This book speaks in the first instance to those who have encountered Christ in his sacraments as they live in The Christian Community. This 'Movement for Religious Renewal' was founded in 1922 by a group of pastors, theologians and students who asked Rudolf Steiner for help in bringing about a renewal in the realm of religious life. As The Christian Community does not publish the words of its sacraments in written form, I shall make references to ritual texts in fragments, assuming that my readers know the larger context, or that they will be tolerant of hearing parts of something they have yet to get to know.

The first part of the book moves through reflections on God, the Trinity, the creation and the existence of evil. The second part describes the life and work of The Christian Community as it helps us towards the new unity, the community. I have tried where I can to bring experiences. These are not meant as illustrations but as one of the sources of the reflection that follows. Where these experiences, which often come at the start of a chapter, are not attributed and written in *italics*, they are my own. What is written is written on my authority. I have learned greatly from my teachers in my training for the priesthood in Stuttgart, Germany, and in my studies for a Bachelor of Divinity in Aberdeen. I acknowledge my debt to my teachers, and acknowledge, too, that mistakes and omissions are entirely due to my own limitations.

*   *   *

Christ reveals himself today in the unique experiences of every striving human soul. Thus the traditional sources of theology in scripture and the tradition of the church come alive when they become part of the suffering and glory of a human biography. Such theology transcends the merely subjective: the experience of one human 'I' resounds with the experiences of others. I hope that these chapters will resonate with the experiences of my readers; and that they may help them to find words that make them, and those to whom they speak, ask: Did not our hearts burn within us?

Part 1. The Experience of God

The holiest visions, visions which carry with them the seal of authority, they all come from the human heart and are therefore subjective. The human heart is often a battlefield where the precious and the vile fight each other. But the human heart can be trusted. It is the heart of man who has been created in the image of God. To man is given authority to speak of God. In man there is something which points beyond man. He can make the one step which lets him stand before God. All he has to do: to return. 'If thou return, and I bring thee back, thou shall stand before me ...'

(Maybaum 1965, p. 87)

1. Where is Your God Now?

Faith in God after the 'death of God'

Letting go

One day, as we returned from work, we saw three gallows ... erected on the *Appelplatz*. Roll call. The SS surrounding us, machine guns aimed at us: the usual ritual. Three prisoners in chains — and, among them, the little *pipel*, the sad-eyed angel. ...

All eyes were on the child. He was pale, almost calm, but he was biting his lips as he stood in the shadow of the gallows. ... the nooses were placed around their necks. ...

'Where is merciful God, where is He?' someone behind me was asking. ...

Then came the march past the victims. The two men were no longer alive. ... But the third rope was still moving: the child, too light, was still breathing. And so he remained for more than half an hour, lingering between life and death, writhing before our eyes. And we were forced to look at him at close range. He was still alive when I passed him. His tongue was still red, his eyes not yet extinguished.

Behind me, I heard the same man asking:

'For God's sake, where is God?'

And from within me, I heard a voice answer:

'Where is He? This is where — hanging here from this gallows ...'

(Wiesel 2006, pp. 64f)

In the twentieth century, the old certainty that God will inter-
vene to prevent the worst from happening was lost. Nowadays,
such certainty seems almost like a historical curiosity when we
encounter it in a document such as the Heidelberg Catechism
(1563), which describes God's providence as follows:

> the almighty and ever-present power of God whereby he
> still upholds, as it were by his own hand, heaven and
> earth together with all creatures, and rules in such a way
> that leaves and grass, rain and drought, fruitful and
> unfruitful years, food and drink, health and sickness,
> riches and poverty, and everything else, come to us not
> by chance but by his fatherly hand.

Today, the scale of suffering we would have to shut out to hold
on to such a belief makes it seem almost blasphemous. If God
controls everything, giving good things to those who deserve
them, and withholding them from those who do not, why is
there so much innocent suffering and injustice in the world?
Where was he in Auschwitz?

The loss of the old image of God's power to protect us can
make us feel lonely and unprotected in an impersonal world.
However, we know that the loss of a preconceived idea is often
a chance to get closer to the truth. Could the 'death of God' turn
out to be not the loss of something real, but only the loss of cherished, but false, ideas? Just as we cannot blame someone for
turning out to be different from our picture of her or him, we
cannot blame God for not being as we had expected or hoped.

The Twenty-Second Psalm describes the situation of the
human soul struggling to come to terms with such a loss. A
thousand years before the coming of Christ, who called out
these words on the Cross, the Psalmist describes a shattering
experience of desertion:

> My God, my God, why hast thou forsaken me?
>   Why art thou so far from helping me, from the words
>   of my groaning?
> O my God, I cry by day, but thou dost not answer;
>   and by night, but find no rest. (verses 1–2)

Three times, the Psalmist falls back on what has carried him in the past. The first time he remembers the faith of his ancestors:

> Yet thou art holy,
>> enthroned on the praises of Israel.
>
> In thee our fathers trusted;
>> they trusted, and thou didst deliver them.
>
> To thee they cried, and were saved;
>> in thee they trusted, and were not disappointed. (3–5)

It is not enough — this confidence deserts him too:

> But I am a worm, and no man;
>> scorned by men, and despised by the people.
>
> All who see me mock at me,
>> they make mouths at me, they wag their heads (6–7)

He falls back on more recent memories: the simple faith of childhood: 'It was you who took me from the womb; you kept me safe on my mother's breast.' (9) However, this gives way to even more terrible experiences:

> Many bulls encompass me,
>> strong bulls of Bashan surround me;
>
> they open wide their mouths at me,
>> like a ravening and roaring lion.
>
> I am poured out like water,
>> and all my bones are out of joint;
>
> my heart is like wax,
>> it is melted within my breast;
>
> my strength is dried up like a potsherd,
>> and my tongue cleaves to my jaws;
>
>> thou dost lay me in the dust of death. (12–15)

In the depths of despair, he calls to God:

> But thou, O LORD, be not far off!
>> O thou my help, hasten to my aid!

> Deliver my soul from the sword,
>   my life from the power of the dog! (19–20)

This cry, wrung from the depths of despair, contains within it the power that transforms the situation:

> I will tell of thy name to my brethren;
>   in the midst of the congregation I will praise thee:
> You who fear the LORD, praise him!
>   all you sons of Jacob, glorify him,
>   and stand in awe of him, all you sons of Israel!
> For he has not despised or abhorred
>   the affliction of the afflicted;
> and he has not hid his face from him,
>   but has heard, when he cried to him. (22–24)

His vision opens for a messianic future:

> All the ends of the earth shall remember
>   and turn to the LORD;
> and all the families of the nations
>   shall worship before him
> ...
>   men shall tell of the LORD to the coming generation,
> and proclaim his deliverance to a people yet unborn,
>   for he has done the deed!
>   (27–31, RSV, adapted)

The Psalmist has found a new power that enables him to sing the song of praise that ends with the affirmation of God's creative and redemptive deed: 'for he has done the deed!'

The faith that he relied on up to this point came from the past, from the world of family and ancestral tradition. The new conviction arises when he lets go of the old. It sounds down the centuries as an answer to the cry that Elie Wiesel heard: Where is God? The answer to this question cannot be abstract. It is the cry of confession wrung from the soul experiencing release from the pain of death and dissolution — 'I shall praise thee!'

This turning point is utterly individual. It makes us free of images of God that in fact shut us off from his reality; we become open to an experience of his being that is at first deep below our consciousness. In children, we can witness this experience in its original form — before there are thoughts to describe it, the child 'knows' that there is God, that she has an angel, that there is good in the world. This is what Jesus means when he says, 'Truly I tell you, whoever does not receive the kingdom of God as a little child will never enter it' (Mark 10:15).

It is this deeply-buried religious feeling that makes passengers pray when their plane hits turbulence. Afterwards they may be embarrassed and dismiss the moment as a superstitious reaction to their fear. The words they used may indeed be superstitious — a plea to be saved by the finger of God — but their deeper content is a cry from the soul that it may be ready to face ultimate reality. Such moments bring us closest to our true beliefs. We come closer to the experience of the Psalmist, to his dismay in the face of dereliction and dissolution — and therefore also to his experience of new life in this death of the soul.

Connecting to this layer of our being does not mean that we turn away in denial from the terrible events of our time. In fact, if we allow these events to be real in our soul along with the thought of God, we will experience no contradiction. If we allow both experiences to stand: dereliction alongside trust in ultimate reality, we discover something about our world. We become aware of the agony of God who in his goodness created the world, and in his love let human beings grow in freedom. The image of the Cross tells us how God bears with his creatures the terrible consequences of this freedom.

God, the ground of being

At eighteen I was sure there was no God. Material theories seemed quite adequate for explaining the universe. It was easy to agree with the popularized Marxism that had come down to me that religion was a deception practised on the underprivileged. I was all the more surprised one spring evening, when I found myself standing on a pathway dappled with the sunlight filtered through birch leaves, saying aloud 'Thank

you, thank you!' I was confused — who was I thanking?
Nevertheless, I was sure that my thanks were meaningful —
that they would be heard.

We cannot explain the world around us with all its beauty and coherence. Neither can we explain our own existence. That I am who I am, is the outcome of myriad factors: I can think back to my parents, their parents: usually after this my images start to get blurred. Then I can continue the chain of thought back through the ages. 'Before that there was the rise of civilization ... before that the first human beings on earth ... before that the formation of our galaxy, and before that the Big Bang.' Nowhere do I reach a final point, a point where I can say: and that's how it all started: that's why I am here now. Even today's cosmology, which can make powerful hypotheses about the beginning of the universe, cannot explain where the universe came from or why it came into being. Why was there a 'singularity' that brought space, time and energy into being, where before there was nothing?

Such reflections can lead us to the thought of One who created the world. This decision to create gives one answer to the great question over which philosophers have puzzled for at least three thousand years: why is there a world and not no world; why is there something and not nothing?

There is a current of thought that goes back to the nineteenth century, which sees in God a projection on to an imaginary figure by ignorant human beings. Now that science can tell us the truth about our origins, and we understand why human beings needed to make up these stories about divine beings to allay their fears and give a focus to their strivings, we can dispense with the idea of God. This view has become very widespread. Any idea of the uniqueness of the human being or any spiritual origin is dismissed as an 'anthropomorphic' (making the world human-shaped) weakness. Even the wish to ask 'why' is dismissed as inappropriate.

Brave though it seems to face being alone in a vast universe of impersonal forces, such thinking nevertheless rests on unquestioned assumptions. Mind, for example, is seen as merely an 'emergent property' — the chance outcome of evolutionary processes that adapted its possessors better to survive to the age where they reproduce. The Stoics — Greek philosophers whose school began three centuries before Christ — had quite a different view of mind, or Logos, as they called it. They recognized that the human capacity for intelligent speech and thought is what links us to the divine Word, through whom the world was created, and whose traces can be seen in the fact that the world is structured in such a way that the little spark of logos within us can grasp it and speak about it.

How could we align this idea with the idea of evolution, which rules out there being any aim towards which everything is moving? One way would be to see the property of logos, the capacity of speech and thought, as something written into the fabric of being like a kind of fundamental force. Just as physical laws cause things to develop in a particular way, there is a law or drive towards the union of spirit and matter, a rational creature who bears within itself the seed of divine substance. The human being then would be an outcome of two forces that are at work: the physically describable mechanisms of evolution by natural selection, and the draw or allure exercised on all creation to develop towards being an expression of divinity.

This means that we have to take our experience of being human more seriously than we are used to. Before the development of scientific and critical thinking in the Enlightenment, and its gradual popularization, it was an unquestioned assumption that man was nature's last word, created in the image of God. This assumption rested on revelation. When fundamentalists today try to read Genesis as a biology textbook, or the proponents of 'intelligent design' try to reconcile evolution with the idea of a creator god, they are still basing what they do on revealed truth. Truly progressive thought however cannot simply bypass the results of scientific investigation. It needs to build upon them. It does this when it reflects on its own nature. The foundation for a spiritual conception of the human being comes from the experience that we all have when we think: we are creators of the world that we think about, which is at the same time real. Through this we experience our dual nature. All that is limited and mistaken in our thinking is the product of our limited nature as incarnate beings. What is objective and true in it shows our connection to a world of objective spiritual being. We are part of a higher order, of the 'kingdom of heaven' as Jesus calls it — and yet we experience that we do not live up to it.

We are faced with what at first seems a paradox. The sovereign freedom of human thinking, which shows that human beings are spiritual beings, led them to reflect upon their own origins with such rigour that they rejected their own spiritual nature, and rejected all idea of there being God. In fact this is no paradox. If we are both free and divinely endowed, we must be able to come to this place.

In any case, the existence of God cannot be proved. Proofs are the result of arguments. In order to argue we have to accept common assumptions. The idea of an ultimate cause is such an assumption: if we think in a materialistic way, we simply assume that there is no explanation. The chain of thought about the origin of things described above simply ends in a question mark, or goes on for ever. Now that cosmology gets closer and closer to describing what it sees as the origin of our universe in the Big Bang, the question of what came before this only becomes more acute. Was there a chain of Big Bangs? What did they occur in — what was there when a previous universe had collapsed, out of which a new one could come about? For the scientific view, however, imagining God as the explanation only makes things more complicated, even if no other explanation has yet been found.

The sage and translator Juan Mascaró (1897–1987) summarizes materialism: 'According to the prosaic view [of the world] all is matter and its energy, and from this somehow comes life and consciousness.' (1993, p. 9) This is the assumption of modern humanity. It was only in the twentieth century that such thoughts became widespread in the broad mass of educated humanity. Now, the thought that we as thinking beings may be alone in the vast universe, that our lives are the result of random chemical and physical reactions, that the idea of a soul or of a personal God are illusions — all this has become everyday, almost banal. We hardly notice any more how desolate the world becomes when we do not see its source in the loving deed of a Creator. More importantly, we do not notice that it flies in the face of our experience as described above.

Few of us have the tools to keep up with modern cosmology, but there is a parallel experience that lies closer to hand. Many people read popular books on psychology. There is a shock when we read that particular childhood experiences lead to attitudes and behaviours that we recognize in ourselves. If we accept the contemporary view of human nature without question, we may feel that this is the explanation of our character. We may however notice a discrepancy with our experience which leaves us uncomfortable. We can accept the descriptions of psychological mechanisms and see their consequences for our behaviour, and such knowledge can help us to become free of them. But our very experience of being able to do this is a demonstration that there is something in us that rises above such mechanisms. We learn from the description of the phenomena, but we do not need to accept the reductionist explanation of human nature that is not read *from* the phenomena but read *into* them. This is an experience of our dual nature. It would be foolish to pretend that we are beings of pure spirit — why then would we need to go through the experiences of growing up in the earthly world? And how else could advertisers and statisticians predict so exactly what most human beings will do in a given situation, with a given stimulus? But our life consists in dealing with our genetic and psychological make-up and fashioning from it a vessel for our true being.

The knowledge of our spiritual nature that comes from such reflection on experience is quite different from the position of one who starts by 'knowing' that we are beings of spirit because of revealed truth. It has a firmer basis precisely because it is grounded in our own experience. No dogma — neither religious nor scientific — has moulded it.

If we carry on with this path of thought, we realize that data about the origins of the universe — which need to be treated with even more scepticism than the results of psychological research, as they rest on layers of hypothetical interpretation of data from the far-distant past — tell us something about the evolution of the material universe; the conclusion that there is not a spiritual dimension is however just a hypothesis, and once again the test of our experience shows it to be unfounded. The resting star in C.S. Lewis's *Voyage of the Dawn Treader,* when he is told that, in the earthly world, stars are only huge balls of flaming gas, says: 'Even in your world, my son, that is not what a star is but only what it is made of' (p. 159).

What difference does it make if God created the world?

The fact that God intended something with his Creation means that all is not random chance. The world around us has a direction, a hope of its development, even if this is not a 'plan' in the sense of something laid down and already decided in the past. We find ourselves on a journey from a beginning to an ultimate end. If we can understand God's purpose in creating, we can begin to understand the purpose of our own lives. Our struggles and strivings are important not only for practical reasons, but they have a wider significance.

In the idea of God's will, his intention, we feel the reality of God as person. Humanity worshipped the spirit in the multiplicity of natural beings for millennia. It was the mission of the ancient Jewish people to wean themselves off the manifoldness of the spiritual in nature and to concentrate on the one within, behind and beyond all the phenomena we can see. Only a single, central being can be thought of truly personally as the author of Creation.

Why did God create the world? In the fourth chapter of the Book of Revelation, the veil is lifted on the state of things before the Creation. There is movement, but it is contained: the glory that the twenty-four elders and the four living creatures send to God returns to them in an unending cycle. The tragedy of this state of affairs is shown in the fifth chapter, when it becomes clear that the story of Creation cannot begin unless something or someone quite different enters the equation. This is the lamb — the one whose sacrifice is at the basis of the whole of Creation. In this image of the lamb already sacrificed we glimpse the great risk that is involved in the act of creating a world with the potential for freedom. It means that God has to limit himself, to allow there to be a world where he is not in control. We have already seen how one result of our freedom is that we can develop a philosophy where there is no God. The purpose and direction of the world is not to run along tracks set down by God before time; much rather, our world is a living dynamic. A power of natural causality drives things and makes them behave predictably. Another force is at work, too, not coercing but drawing creation on — 'alluring' us, to use the word used by John Taylor.[3] This is the Holy Spirit, who mysteriously makes all that is part of the plan whose full dimensions and fulfilment are in the future, and which draws creation forward to choice, selfhood and creative, self-giving love.

In the contrast between the fourth chapter of the Book of Revelation and what follows, we gain an insight into God's reasons for creating. God longs for community and, surprising as it may seem, for conversation. This means that there must be a part of creation that is truly free, for only when free beings turn in love to their Creator — when they take up his offer of conversation — is God's longing fulfilled. Conversation with perfect mirrors or puppets is no conversation at all.

The idea of God as a conversation partner, longing for community, is already present in the Hebrew Bible. Most people who have had any religious instruction will remember the dominant image of the relationship between God and man in the Hebrew Bible as the covenant or treaty, an agreement regulated by law. It is remarkable however, that God is not a strict covenant-partner. Although he threatens terrible retribution if the Israelites do not keep their side of the bargain, he is prepared ever and again to forgive their betrayals of the covenant. In one of the most moving passages of the Hebrew Bible, God assumes the part of a husband who is going out to woo his faithless wife, to re-establish their marriage:

> Therefore, behold, I will allure her,
>   and bring her into the wilderness,
>   and speak tenderly to her.
> And there I will give her vineyards,
>   and make the Valley of Achor a door of hope.
> And there she shall answer as in the days of her youth,
>   as at the time when she came out of the land of Egypt.
> And in that day, says the LORD, you will call me, 'My

husband,' and no longer will you call me, 'My Baal.' And I will betroth you to me for ever; I will betroth you to me in righteousness and in justice, in steadfast love, and in mercy. I will betroth you to me in faithfulness; and you shall know the LORD.

(Hosea 2:14–20, RSV)

If we let these images live in us, we can feel the reality of God as person. Just as we could not be human if we could not hope, we realize that hope for his creation is central to God's creative being. His power does not lie in coercion — here the scientific world-view protects us from an old error about God. There is no space for the kind of directing will that creationists want to uphold in the working of natural laws. In fact, it takes us much closer to the mystery of God if we see that he seeks to persuade, to 'allure' us into communion with him. To pray to this God is not the same as petitioning an angry tyrant, who may or may not grant us our request. In prayer we seek to align ourselves with his purposes in creation.

Russian Orthodox theology gives another image for the origin of creation. It sees in the fourth chapter of the Book of Revelation a 'circulation of glory.' At the beginning of things, this circulation was perfect, but it was limited. In creation, the glory spilled over into a world which was not only glory. Our task as human beings is to restore the circulation by giving glory to God — by making all that we do sacramental.[4] The Hassidic Jews knew this too: they saw in every earthly phenomenon a spark of the original glory. The pious man — the Hassid — releases these sparks from every thing he touches, and every thought he thinks. When he walks, he leaves behind him a trail of footsteps like little pools of fire. When the pious assemble to pray, it is like a great bonfire whose sparks fly up into the night sky.[5] When we pray 'hallowed be thy name,' we are praying that the divine spark at the centre of every thing be released by the way we live.

I once stood in an art gallery looking at the first abstract pictures, painted by Wassily Kandinsky just before the First World War. It dawned on me that these pictures — not based

*on observation of the external world, the first creation — mark
a new stage in the conversation between God and humanity.
For in them, the original, creative spirit of human beings manifests itself. Sparks of creativity and beauty are liberated and
fly into the heaven to join the praise of the angels and all the
beings of the hierarchies who have never ceased praising God
since the very beginning of things.*

To pray 'Thy kingdom come' is not to ask for a sudden eruption
from another world, the 'God in the machine' wheeled on at the
end of a Greek tragedy. We ask God to give us strength so that
we can take responsibility for the kingdom ourselves. We pray
that we may recognize in the kingdom of Creation the divine
name in every thing; we foster love to creation and creativity in
each other; we pray that we may live by values that echo God's
purposes in creation — that we become ever more worthy dialogue partners for God. Praying in this way means we must be
prepared to take up the burden of living the Kingdom in the
world with all its beauty and goodness and all its evil. We do not
pray for God to abolish evil, but to give us strength to become
his partners in meeting it.

2. The Trinity — a doctrine born of experience

Images of God as controlling monarch and distant judge do not help us to deal with the reality of our world. Nor do they bring us closer to the personal God, who longs for communion with human beings. If these images obscure the truth, where can we find images that bring us closer to his true being? The images that can help us here are those of God as Trinity.

The most abstract formulation of the doctrine of the Trinity states that God is three divine persons who share one divine nature. At first sight, this seems to sum up the remoteness of official doctrine from the world of ordinary people. How can quibbling about the make-up of God's being be relevant to my needs as a human being, or to my praying? In the first chapter, we noted how at the birth of modern theology, Friedrich Schleiermacher relegated his discussion of the Trinity to the end of his *Christian Faith*. It seems far less important than the discussion of religion rooted in human experience. Many Christians today are heirs of Schleiermacher: they see their belief in God as far more important than abstract speculations on his nature. This makes it all the more remarkable to discover that this doctrine itself has its origin in a deeply felt experience at the very beginning of Christianity.

> Eight days later, his disciples were again in the house, and Thomas was with them. The doors were shut, but Jesus came and stood among them, and said, 'Peace be with you.' Then he said to Thomas, 'Put your finger here, and see my hands; and put out your hand, and place it in my side; do not be faithless, but believing.' Thomas answered him, 'My Lord and my God!' (John 20:26–28)

When Thomas addresses the Risen Christ as Lord and God, he is giving voice to a powerful experience. Four centuries later, Christians were only just beginning to understand this experience. Even today, we are hardly beyond the beginning. At first, the experience that in Jesus, God is on the earth, was so intense and alive that there was no need to formulate belief in an abstract way. Later, the revolutionary nature of Thomas' experience started to become clear. We can understand this if we compare Thomas' confession with the first and most fundamental commandment given to the Jewish people through Moses:

> I am the LORD your God, who brought you out of the land of Egypt, out of the house of bondage. You shall have no other gods before me. (Exodus 20:2–3, RSV)

Even more emphatic are the words from the so-called 'Sh'ma Yisrael,' the 'Hear O Israel' from the Book of Deuteronomy which are recited every morning and evening by pious Jews:

> Hear O Israel, the Lord is our God, the Lord is one! (6:4)

For twenty centuries, the Jewish people had had the task of grasping the oneness of God. We only have to recall their path through the desert after the Exodus to see how hard this was. In the very moment when God revealed himself to Moses on the mountain top, the Israelites erected a golden calf and worshipped it as a god, in orgiastic ecstasy. It was a hard cultural task, to turn the attention of a nation away from the multiplicity of spiritual beings at work in the world, to the underlying unity of all things, which is at first the greatest abstraction. Yet it was necessary for human beings if they were ever to separate themselves from the powers of nature, and to experience their own unitary nature as beings endowed with an 'I.' This achievement could not be undone by the new experience of God in Jesus Christ.

So what does it mean when Thomas calls Jesus 'my God'? Has the one God himself come down to the earth as Jesus? Is Jesus a 'second god'? Or is Jesus not really God, but an exceptional human being, whom Thomas is honouring with the title of God?

When theologians began to account for Christian belief to the wider world (in a form of writing called *Apology*, meaning a defence of their faith), they drew on the resources of contemporary philosophy. This was still rooted in the background of the ancient mysteries. The dual background in mystery and philosophical thought is particularly clear in the case of the idea of Christ as the *Logos* or word drawn from the language of the Stoic philosophy. We can experience the mystery of the Word through a simple meditation on our humanity. What distinguishes us from the animals? Perhaps the most important aspect is our capacity for speech, for conveying thoughts. Nowadays we speak of the genus of humanity as 'man the knower' (*homo sapiens*); we could just as well speak of man the speaker, *homo loquens*. The Hebrew word for animal, *behemah*, means mute — by implication, human beings are the creatures that speak.

The being of the Word had been the content of the mysteries and the meditations of humanity for millennia. The word is the epitome of human beings' spiritual nature and creativity. In speaking, human beings show that they are partly divine. In the Hellenistic world — the culture that emerged in the Eastern Mediterranean following the conquests of Alexander the Great — Jewish thinkers developed a philosophy that drew on the Old Testament and Greek thinking. They saw the connection between Greek thinking about the Logos and the Book of Genesis, in which God 'speaks' the world into being. By the time of Christ, philosophers had started to see God's Word in creation not merely as a fleeting utterance of God, but as a being in its own right, derived from God but distinct from Him. In this way, two great mysteries about God's being could be reconciled: his utter transcendence — his separateness from the world — and his presence as a power in the world.

Greek philosophy grasped the truth that God is utterly distinct from the world. In the *via negativa* (the negative way), thinkers saw a way to apprehend God's being through contemplating his opposite. The world is subject to change; God is changeless. We human beings are subject to passions; God is passionless — and so on. Through this way of contemplation, we arrive at the conception of God as the Unmoved Mover, the unchanging Ground of Existence.

However, if God is so utterly remote from our world, which is subject to time and change, how can he be responsible for its creation? How can the timeless, unchanging God work into a world of time and change? In some of their wilder speculations, Gnostic groups around the time of Christ had suggested that the material world was not the work of the God, but of an evil *demiurge,* an inferior spiritual being, who wished to trap humanity in the snare of matter. The first Christian theologians rightly realized that this contradicted the whole mystery of Christianity. Christ came, not to liberate human beings from the earth, but to save them *in* the earth, and with them to save the earth itself. The mystery of the divine Logos built a bridge from God's transcendence to his involvement in the world. The creative will of the Unmoved Mover comes to expression through God's Word.

Origen taught that the Word is born eternally from God. There was never a time when God was without his word, through whom creation came into existence. However, he left the implications unclear, drawing more upon his living experience than abstract argumentation. If the Word is a 'second God,' as he sometimes says, how can we still affirm the oneness of God?

The fourth century

In the fourth century, the uncritical relationship to spiritual truths that characterized the first period of Christian theology was passing away. Where there had been an holistic vision, there was now the tendency to abstraction, which splits and splinters truth.

This is the background to the dispute that occupied the church for most of the fourth century, the dispute between Arius and his followers and Athanasius and his.

Each of these teachers apprehended a vital part of the conception of God. Arius saw Christ at work as the creator spirit in the world. He is the divine Logos, the agent of the immovable, unchanging god of Greek thought in this world of change and development. He belongs to the created order, as the 'first born of all creation.' As first-born he was born before time or as the beginning of time itself. Because he is part of our created world he is our brother, albeit far greater than we are. He is part of the community of creation.

Athanasius, Arius' opponent, grasped the closeness of the Son to the Father. He saw that the mystery of the Trinity, implicit in Thomas' confession, cannot be solved by putting a second god alongside the Father; much rather, it gives us a glimpse into the inner being of God-self. In one of the deathblows to Arian theology, Athanasius points out that if the Son were created, we would be idolaters when we worship Christ, as we know that we are not to worship anything other than God himself. If we experience Christ as a person in his own right, then we cannot start to think of second gods or majestic creatures; much rather, we must change our idea of Godhead, seeing a community of divine persons in one divine nature.

The tragedy of the dispute between Arianism and the orthodox theology that emerged is that one side had to be victorious. Both Arius and Athanasius had grasped an aspect of the truth about God. There is both a created and an uncreated Logos. The divine Logos or Son-God has a counterpart in creation, a logos who is created as his reflection in the world of space and time. This 'created logos' is the totality of the beings of the Hierarchies, the members of God's being, and his agents in creation. When thinking of Jesus Christ we do not have to make an 'either/or' decision about the divine being who incarnates in him, created or uncreated; rather, we can see the working of both principles in the incarnation. This means that there is community of divinity and humanity within Christ himself — or, to use the philosophical language of the early church, he is consubstantial — *homoousios* — both with God and with us.[6]

The Christian church adopted Trinitarian theology after the long struggles that culminated in the Council of Constantinople in 381. However, many Christians then being converted were drawn to Arian Christianity, above all the Germanic tribes who were gradually infiltrating Europe as the Roman Empire declined. Arianism embodied an element that appealed to these peoples who had not passed through the centuries of cultural development that the peoples of the classical world had experienced. They were still deeply connected with the world of the elements, the world of creation. They found in the Christianity of Arius what in modern times is called 'the cosmic Christ.' Christ is not a far distant part of Godhead, but the creative principle in the world and in man.

The image of God

I once attended a meeting to plan a conference where we started with nothing but an idea of the title. We each spoke about what the theme meant to us, about which new aspects were important. Somehow it happened: we stopped only hearing ourselves, stopped waiting to have our say, as so often happens in meetings. Suddenly we were in a dance — each contributing what they could give, hardly noticing whether it was I or another who had spoken. There was a risk involved — would we be finished with our discussion in time to make a decision? We had to put all tensions and worries on one side. When our conversation was over, we looked at each other almost shyly, in wonder. Something had happened for which we hardly had words. Out of our conversation, a clear idea of the content of the conference had emerged. Each had forgotten him or herself, and in forgetting, had come far closer to him or herself.

Our deepest experience of being human comes from our being in relation, not in isolation. We all know the kind of conversation where we can't wait for the other person to stop speaking, so that we can get a word in edgeways. And we know too the kind of communion that can come about when we overcome this egotistical kind of listening. A current of communication flows between us; we nourish each other with our words.

However, even those whose work or existence is solitary are in a kind of conversation. The artist who withdraws in order to paint or sculpt is in a dialogue with his or her fellow artists, present and past, and with those who will see the work when it is completed. The hermit prays for the world, even if he has removed himself from it.

We have seen how the experience of God in Jesus Christ led

Christians to perceive that God is not a single person, but a unity of three persons. Augustine speaks of the Trinity as the lover, the beloved and the love that unites them. The Father is the lover, the son the beloved and the Spirit is the bond of love between them. We cannot imagine the lover without the object of his love; we cannot imagine the beloved without the love that makes him beloved; we cannot imagine either without the love that is their bond. Each 'person' of the Trinity bestows being on the other by what they *do:* giving love, receiving love, and uniting.

An image from Greek Orthodox thought adds another aspect. Here, the Trinity is the divine dance, the *perichoresis.* Three dancers circle together in time with the music. They are separate individuals; through their joining together, something that exists over and above each one as an individual is born: the dance itself. At the heart of the universe is the dance of love within Godhead. The power of love that animates the dance is not inward-turned. It spills over in creation. The unity of God becomes multiplicity.

In the 'farewell discourses,' Jesus reveals that the dance is not over, and that for God, there are never enough partners in the dance. We are to go along the way that Jesus prepares for us, the 'way to the Father.' Father and Son are also on their way to us, where they will remain. We are to join in the dance so that creation may carry on in our dancing.

Created for community

The first creation of the *adam* — the Hebrew word for 'human being,' not yet a proper name — creates a single being.[7] 'Male and female he created him,' says the text — that is to say, the original human being is sexless, or rather he/she unites the sexes; it is a hermaphrodite. Duality is contained within one being.

In a second step of creation, the human being is fashioned not only in spirit but from the dust of the earth. He/she is created single, of one kind. Then something quite extraordinary happens. Up until now, God has reviewed his creation and found it 'good' or 'very good.' Now, he looks at the human being he has created and says: 'It is not good that the human being should be alone' (2:18). God has created something that is not good! We can perhaps understand this in the sense that it is not perfect, not finished. In the human being God has something which is at the beginning, not at the end of its journey.

And now God tries a whole range of things to make good what is 'not good.' He creates the kingdoms of nature, but these are not enough to overcome the singleness of the human being. There is a kind of pathos in God's attempts:

> So out of the ground the LORD God formed every beast of the field and every bird of the air, and brought them to the human being to see what it would call them; and whatever the human being called every living creature, that was its name. The human being gave names to all cattle, and to the birds of the air, and to every beast of the field; but for the human being there was not found a helper. (2:19, RSV modified)

There is too much difference between the human being and the other kingdoms of nature; *Adam* can name them, but they cannot be 'helpers.' At first reading, we might wonder how realistic this is; after all, the domesticated animals have been the helpers of humanity since time immemorial. But we realize that it is a deeper kind of help that is meant here. A helper is not a mere executor of the will of another, but one who enters into the purposes of the other. A deeper communion, a deeper sharing of intentions is part of God's purpose for humanity. Now God takes the next step: instead of creating more beings outside the human being, he brings about a differentiation *within* the unitary human being:

> So the LORD God caused a deep sleep to fall upon the human being, and while he slept took one of its ribs and closed up the place with flesh; and the rib which the LORD God had taken from the human being he made into a woman and brought her to the human being. Then Adam said, 'This at last is bone of my bones and flesh of my flesh; she shall be called Woman, because she was

taken out of Man.' Therefore shall a man leave his father
and his mother, and shall cleave unto his wife: and they
shall be one flesh.
(2:23, RSV modified)

The image is fascinating if we overcome the centuries' old mis-
interpretation that the original human being was a man, and the
woman is somehow derived from him in secondary way. The
singleness of the human being was 'not good.' Now, there has
been a differentiation — there are now two beings that share the
same human nature.

Through the division, something quite new is possible.
'Therefore shall a man leave his father and his mother, and shall
cleave unto his wife: and they shall be one flesh' (2:24). Through
the division, a new unity is possible — a new aim for the human
being. This is possible through the kind of 'help' that God
wishes for. It is not enough that human beings become separate,
merely to exist alongside each other. They fulfil God's purpose
in helping each other. In this way they will join in a higher unity.

This journey of human development echoes the journey of
the whole of creation — from unity to separateness to a higher
unity, to community.

Now the story of humanity begins. The story unfolds without pause until the fulfilment in the Book of Revelation. But here
a kind of echo of the Creation comes, when the image of the new
unity between heaven and earth is symbolized in the image of
the marriage. The process of creation itself is repeated on a
human scale. Godself overflows into the world, which is separate from God. The aim of all of creation, its underlying tendency, is to achieve union with God. But this is no mere return,
which annuls what has happened through the separation; the
final unity is infinitely enriched by all that went before. This
insight, that God himself changes by going through the development of his creation, is expressed in the Advent prayer of the
Act of Consecration of Man, which speaks of the 'becoming' of
human beings, in which the becoming of God is contained.

Here again we see how vulnerable God makes himself in creation. Far safer to stay in the enclosed circulation of glory of
Revelation 4! The whole mystery of freedom, evil and commun-

ion is contained in the paradox that for the higher communion to come about, creation needs to be given the power to reject communion altogether.

Does this not contradict one of the most powerful paradigms that make up our mental landscape: that we need to grow out of childish dependence and become separate, independent beings? Two thousand years of history prepared the Jews to believe in the oneness of God. Similarly, half a millennium of history, the time since the Renaissance and Reformation, has prepared modern humanity to believe in the oneness of the self. The revolutionary power of the image of the Trinity is that it shows us that this idea of the isolated self is only a stage on a longer journey.

The image as archetype

In the Book of Genesis, God says, 'Let us create the human being in our image; after our likeness let us make it' (1:26). Irenaeus, the Christian theologian of the second century (ca. 140–202), saw the 'image' as the fundamental character of the human being. The 'likeness' is what we have to strive towards. The earth is the place where this striving is possible, through the adversity and the resistance that we encounter. The experience that every striving human being has, that there is a discrepancy between what I am as a given and what I sense I could become, is an experience of the difference between image and likeness.

In *Peer Gynt*, the epic drama written by Henrik Ibsen (1826–1906), the trolls represent the human being as the product only of natural evolution. Their proud motto is: 'To your own self be enough!' They confront Peer with what human beings are when they have no purpose that reaches beyond themselves. Peer, who is a great adventurer and fantasist, finally has to recognize that in his whole career he has not developed himself at all, because he has run away from the challenges that would have cracked open the hard shell of himself. He has not lived up to the motto that he tells the trolls is the essence of humanity: 'To your own self be true!' Many people feel the danger of living a life that has no horizon beyond the everyday grind, and they write 'mission statements' for themselves. Artificial as this can be, it springs from the desire to embody an 'image' in life that is not immediately given.

But how do we find the image towards which we might strive? A meditation on what forms us soon makes us realize that everything fine and good about us came from being connected to other human beings. We come to understand ever more about the vital role that the family and early education play in the formation of children's character. Each of us can probably remember a favourite teacher who inspired us with love for a subject. As we make our way through life, our spouse, our friends and colleagues give us the reflection, the affirmation and support that we need to become our best selves. This resonates with the image of God as Trinity. If God is a lonely eminence, a distant monarch arbitrarily judging and condemning, ruling his 'subjects,' then our aim must ultimately be to become like this. If on the other hand we see God as a community of persons, bestowing being and substance upon each other in a creative dance, then such communal being must be our aim. The social structures that we create can be seen to be closer or further from this ideal. We will look for structures that enable the 'dance,' the communal sharing and bestowing of being as we work together. Rigid power-structures with a clear hierarchy, which ironically enough are often created with the aim of protecting divinely-sanctioned truths, have not yet been imbued with the image of the Trinity. Our challenge is to create structures that further the creative potential of every human encounter, making it open for the invitation to the dance of overflowing, self-bestowing creativity that underlies the whole of creation.

We discover here the deeper reason behind a fact of our psychology. Human beings are most fulfilled when they can give themselves to some aim outside of themselves. It is becoming ever clearer that the rise in affluence does not lead to a society of happy, fulfilled human beings. Once a certain level of prosperity has been reached — when creature comforts are supplied to a level which means that the whole of life does not need to be devoted simply to subsisting — any additional rise in prosperity does not make people more fulfilled. What does, is being able to give oneself to an end with which one can identify.[8] For many people, the moment when this first becomes real for them is when they have children. But there are innumerable ways to give ourselves — what is clear is that in this lies the only hope of wholeness and fulfilment.

This brings us closer to understanding a phrase from the New Testament that many people find hard to understand, the so-called 'blasphemy against the Holy Spirit' which will not be forgiven. It is through the Holy Spirit that we can be reconnected to the overflowing abundance of God. When we deny this connection — not necessarily in thought, but in deeds — then we deny the foundation of our own being. We cut ourselves off at the root.

This does not mean that there is no differentiation within structures that further the life of creative, self-giving love. It is a mistake made on the other side of the spectrum, to reduce everyone and everything to one level. In fact, the Trinity is a lesson in how differentiation makes a true cooperation possible, even to the level of the union of substance that we see in the Trinity.

3. The Wounded Healer

Superhero

A remarkable book appeared in America in 1999 and quickly became a bestseller. *Expecting Adam,* by Martha Beck, tells 'the story of two driven Harvard academics who found out mid-pregnancy that their child was retarded ... They decided to allow their baby to be born.' The book describes how they gradually realize that 'they themselves were the ones who would be "born," infants in a new world where magic is commonplace. Harvard professors are slow learners, and retarded babies are the master teachers.'

Martha Beck describes both the fear and disappointment, and the anxiety for her child's well being that grow in her after the discovery. In the end, however, she realizes that her greatest concern was not for him but for herself:

> What my fears all boiled down to, as I sat with my tiny orange son in the days after his birth, was an underlying terror that he would destroy my own facade, the flawlessness and invulnerability I projected on to the big screen, the Great and Terrible Martha of Oz. You see, I knew all along that there wasn't one label people might apply to Adam — stupid, ugly, strange, clumsy, slow, inept — that could not, at one time or another, be justifiably applied to me. I had spent my life running from this catastrophe, and like so many other things, it caught up with me while I was expecting Adam. (p. 316)

The life-changing event of bearing this child challenged her deepest values, and made her change her idea of what the good life is.

In this regard, as in so many others, my worst fears have come to pass. But as they do I am learning that there is an even bigger secret, a secret I had been keeping from myself. It has been hard for me to grasp, but gradually, painfully, with the slow, small steps of a retarded child, I am coming to understand it. This has been the second phase of my education, the one that followed all those years of school. In it, I have had to unlearn virtually everything Harvard taught me about what is precious and what is garbage. I have discovered that many of the things I thought were priceless are as cheap as costume jewellery, and much of what I labelled worthless was, all the time, filled with the kind of beauty that directly nourishes my soul.

Now I think that the vast majority of us 'normal' people spend our lives trashing our treasures and treasuring our trash. We bustle around trying to create the impression that we are hip, imperturbable, omniscient, in perfect control, when in fact we are awkward and scared and bewildered. The irony is that we do this to be loved, all the time remaining terrified of anyone who seems to be as perfect as we wish to be.

Living with Adam, loving Adam, has taught me a lot about the truth. (p. 317)

The power of the book comes in part from Martha Beck's honesty, and in part from the fact that a Harvard professor is a symbol, a cultural icon that embodies what we value most. We see a person with education, money, power and influence as having the good life. We want such a life for ourselves and for our children. We want to be protected from pain and suffering, to be beyond danger. We are uneasily aware that we cannot hold death and illness at bay, along with the loss of control they bring, but we act as if we could. This is the brittle façade that Martha Beck describes; a kind of perversion of values that comes from wrong priorities.

There is another cultural icon that embodies these values: the 'superhero' of modern action films. The superheroes such as Batman, Superman and Spiderman struggle for the good against forces of evil that seem set to overwhelm the world. Through their strength and ingenuity they can deliver the world from any problem, any evil that besets it. We recognize the world that these films show, but it has a crucial difference from ours. For all that we glorify strength and achievement, we know that there are problems that we are unable to solve with our powers. The superheroes can deal with any problems. In their world, we can be saved from the random madness of suicidal terrorism, the threat of destruction by nuclear weapons or the impact of an asteroid. This make-believe world is itself only a projection of our façade and its message is ultimately despairing.

Batman begins with a portrayal of Gotham City, a future dystopic New York, in which evil holds sway. The forces that should be protecting the innocent — the politicians and police — have been corrupted; good individuals are pawns at the mercy of the powers of evil. Only Batman, who is blessed with unearthly powers, has the power to do battle with the Joker, the diabolical embodiment of nihilistic power. The ending of *Batman* is desolate: after his victory, Batman leaves the adoring crowd. They are the same as they were before; nothing has happened that has made these people or their society better able to meet evil when it next arises. There is no reason to think that evil will not grow up again. We can only hope that Batman does not go too far away!

The superhero films glorify their heroes. They are shown to be strong, victorious and honourable. They are messiahs, bringers of salvation. But their victory and honour cheat the true messianic hope because they are projections of a distorted image of the human. We cannot wish to become Batman: in fact, he is defined by being other than us, alien. He does not share in our plight as human beings. His glorious victory over evil leaves an aftertaste of nihilistic despair.

Christ the hero

There is an unnerving similarity between *Batman* and the other superhero films and some popular Christian theology. Christ is the otherworldly visitor who does battle with the forces of evil and vanquishes them before returning to Heaven. Unlike

Batman, the film does not end after he leaves. The fact that the world is still in the grip of powerful forces of evil has to be explained, and this can be done in various ways: we may hope to follow Christ in his escape from this world; or we may hope for the Millennium, when all wrongs will be put right and a kingdom of justice and peace will be established by Christ when he returns. Christ is the supreme achiever who will eventually overcome all problems.

This popular Christian theology is also pessimistic about the world. Human beings are not changed. They have been 'saved,' transferred from the state of damnation to a new status of salvation. They have not developed, so that one could hope that they might start to meet evil — which is still all too evident in the world — in a new, creative way. The otherness of Christ and his subsequent absence mean desolation for human beings. Their destiny on the earth is hopeless.

Pioneering thinkers of the modern era rejected this kind of theology. Ludwig Feuerbach saw religion as immature. God and the gods are merely the projections of naïve human beings who take the best qualities of the human and concentrate them in a supreme being who becomes the object of human longing. We do not need the thought of the Spirit to appreciate the supremacy of man. When human beings liberate themselves from childish fairy-tale pictures, nothing will stand in the way of their realizing their god-like potential. Feuerbach's message was optimistic and liberating: once human beings grasp their potential, they will have untold power to release the world from the forces of sin and corruption.

Karl Marx was moved by the compassion he felt with those who were being abused and disregarded by the emerging industrial societies of the West. The churches of Western Europe had failed to see their Christian task in relation to the dehumanizing conditions of industrialized societies, and whole populations were left without spiritual or physical nourishment. Marx saw in religion a distraction and diversion of our limited human resources that should be used to achieve social justice.

Looking back on the secular totalitarian systems of the twentieth century, we can see that it was not so easy to build a brave new world with purely human powers. Their tyrants embodied an image of humanity as invulnerable and omnipotent. Their descent into demonic nihilism shows what happens when this image becomes an idol.

The hope of the Messiah

The Jewish people developed the idea of the Messiah in a rich tapestry of images, which grew over two millennia. In one of the most beautiful passages of the Bible, Isaiah speaks of the coming of a 'servant of the Lord':

> As many were astonished at him — his appearance was so marred, beyond human semblance, and his form beyond that of the sons of men — so shall he startle many nations; kings shall shut their mouths because of him; for that which has not been told them they shall see, and that which they have not heard they shall understand.

Only those who are open for something new and unexpected can grasp what is meant.

> Who has believed what we have heard? And to whom has the arm of the LORD been revealed?
> For he grew up before him like a young plant, and like a root out of dry ground; he had no form or comeliness that we should look at him, and no beauty that we should desire him. He was despised and rejected by men; a man of sorrows, and acquainted with grief; and as one from whom men hide their faces he was despised, and we esteemed him not. Surely he has borne our griefs and carried our sorrows; yet we esteemed him stricken, smitten by God, and afflicted.

One by one, our assumptions are held up and overturned. We have already seen how for many people, living a good life means being successful and attractive, well thought of, and enjoying comfort. Even idealists prize effectiveness and power, used of course for noble ends. Like the friends of Job, we see in affliction the just deserts of sin. In deepest irony, Isaiah convicts us of dismissing the one who brought salvation as unloved by God. The prophecy reaches its climax:

> But he was wounded for our transgressions, he was bruised for our iniquities; upon him was the chastisement that made us whole, and by his wounds we are healed.
> (Isaiah 52:13–53:12, RSV, altered)

In action films the hero often faces the final showdown at some terrible disadvantage, handicapped by an injury or some finer feeling that prevents him acting as forcefully as his unscrupulous adversary. However, he triumphs in spite of the setback — his strength is greater than his wounds. The wounds of the Wounded Healer are quite different. A writer on pastoral care used the following words to describe wounds:

> A wound is an opening in the walls of our body, a breaking of the barrier between us and the world around us. ... [it] is 'a passage through which we may become infected and also through which we affect others.' Naturally, then, we view wounds with distaste and alarm. The sight of blood and of gaping flesh creates sensations of nausea and fear in us, because it warns of pain, permanent damage to the body and the spread of infection. Our instinct for self-preservation leads us to avoid wounds whenever possible and, when they are sustained, to seek immediate remedy.
>
> Yet paradoxically our fear and nausea would be much greater if we encountered a body which could not bleed, could not be wounded. Blood is a sign of life for us and the softness of skin and flesh reveals humanity. (Hence the poignancy of Shylock the Jew's question: 'If you prick us, do we not bleed ... If you poison us, do we not die?') This means that open wounds and flowing blood evoke other associations: the break in the body's walls can bring the wounded person closer to us. We respond to vulnerability, seeing before us 'a fellow creature in

pain.' Thus blood and wounds have important positive effects in creating a sense of community. The opening in the body is a channel of communication from one isolated individual to another; the hazardous outflowing of blood an ultimate risking of the self for others. ...

... Surprisingly, then, wounds, which seem at first frightening and nauseating, can also be 'open and beautiful.' For wounds reveal that fine boundary between living and dying, which makes human life so precious and so revered. (Alistair Campbell 1986, p. 40)

Our vulnerability is our humanity. Without it we may stand alongside each other, but there is no true encounter. In the superhero film *Terminator* we see the android peel back his skin and take out the bullets from his arm, and we feel the horror of invulnerability that Alistair Campbell describes.

The disturbing image of the Wounded Healer reveals a deep truth: the superheroes are inhuman in their invulnerability. Ultimately, they cannot cure the situation. Their promise is counterfeit; as much as we long for the delusion they offer, we know deep inside that only a human healer, a wounded healer can help, as we know deep inside that we can only become ourselves through our vulnerability. Adam, the infinitely vulnerable child of the successful Harvard academics, is a far truer image of the human than the superheroes; his vulnerability shows us what the vulnerability of our saviour must be like.

All of this shows that there must be a community between us and the one who is to save us. The dry doctrine that Jesus Christ shares our nature, as well as being divine, covers over a living truth — only one who bleeds when he is cut shares our being enough that the salvation he brings can change our humanity. The counterpart of the machine peeling back the flesh to pick bullets from its mechanical arm is the one who appears and opens his arms to Thomas, and in a gesture of utter vulnerability says to him: 'See ... put your hand in my side ...' The depth of the mystery of the God-Man opens up before us: Thomas' statement 'My Lord and my God' is a reaction not to an epiphany of power, but to the wounds of the God who went through death.

4. Truly God and Truly Man

It is I, I,
I lay between you, I was
open, was
audible, ticked at you, your breathing
obeyed, it is
I still, but then
you are asleep.
(Celan 1980, p. 60)

The central belief of Christianity, that in Jesus Christ God became man, seems to be a paradox. Human and divine realities seem to be a contrasting pair. For the Incarnation to have done something for human beings that they could not do themselves, it is vital that something more than human entered history. But for the Incarnation to be real and not a mere visit by a god from above in disguise, this divine being must have become truly human. The paradox of the God-man has been a challenge for Christians from the very beginning of Christianity. In the gospels we hear the reactions of those who saw the man, Jesus, in front of them. Some of them knew his parents. How could they believe, when confronted with a man, that God is at work in him? How can it be right to say of him, as Thomas does at the very end of the Gospel story: 'My Lord and my God'? After Ascension, the disciples experienced a different side of the paradox. They experienced the power of the ascended Lord and struggled to understand how it could be true to say that this power came from one who had been and somehow was still human.

Paul summed up the central problem of Christian theology in his Letter to the Corinthians when he said: 'I preach Christ

crucified, a scandal to the Jews and foolishness to the Greeks'
(1 Corinthians 1:23). The scandal of Christ is not his humanity —
the Jews expected a glorified human Messiah — but the *kind* of
humanity, most crucially his death on the cross. The Jews held
that he who 'dies on the tree' is 'cursed' (Galatians 3:13). They
were waiting for a powerful Messiah-King who would restore
the empire of David and the honour of Israel, ushering in an age
where God's values would be achieved miraculously on the
physical plane. It is hardly possible to imagine a greater contrast
with the message of a human messiah who died the disgraceful
death of a common criminal, naked and exposed on the cross.

The 'foolishness' of the Gospel message is that it states that
God can truly become man even to the point of dying. For the
Greeks — the philosophers of the age — this sentence is non-
sense. God is everything that human beings are not: eternal and
unchanging, all-powerful, all-knowing. He belongs to a completely different order of things. It is not only hard to imagine
that he would ever want to become man; it is impossible and
ridiculous.

Understanding the extremes

The development of theology in the first centuries of
Christianity is an impassioned groping towards understanding,
rather like a lover's attempt to account for his love. At the beginning of theology was a deeply-felt experience. Christ had done
something for humanity and the world that changed everything. But who was he? What had he done? Why had it been
necessary? And how did he bring it about? Finding clear
answers meant much soul-searching.

As often happens when we try to explain what matters most
to us, theologians became one-sided in their thoughts. Thus
'heresies' emerged, one-sided attempts to resolve the paradox of
the God-man. There were those who said that Jesus was a
simple man who had fulfilled the messianic hope of the Hebrew
Scriptures. Their response was the same as those who knew his
parents. In the fourth century, Arius also saw Christ's closeness
to us. He is a brother creature, one far greater but of the same

order of being as man. But to fix Christ in one place, so close to humanity, was one-sided. Along with the comforting closeness of Christ, Christians experience something different in their worship. Through Christ, they know that they can enter into relation with ultimate reality, with God — not merely with a higher order of created being. Out of the struggle to do justice to this experience, the doctrine of the Trinity emerged, as we saw above.

Other theologians were passionately committed to articulating their experience of the divinity of Christ. Saint John had said: 'And the Word was God.' The Gospels were full of stories of his wonders, his healings, and his supernatural knowledge. How easy to affirm then, that he only *seemed* to be man. These heresies — called *docetic*, from the Greek 'to appear' — could not encompass Jesus Christ's humanity. This was seen as a mere semblance, a disguise that he had assumed in order to remain hidden on the earth. Before the crisis of the Crucifixion he escaped back to heaven.

The two heresies were rejected, but the two tendencies they represented remained in the great schools of theology roughly grouped around the important cities of Alexandria and Antioch in the early centuries. The Alexandrian school emphasized Christ's divinity. This divinity had assumed 'flesh,' the carapace of a human being. The theologian Apollinaris (died 390) thought this through to its extreme. His picture of the Incarnation was that Christ replaced the *nous*, the intellectual seat of initiative, the centre of the personality of Jesus Christ. Only if this were true could Christ have lived a perfect life, unsullied by the impure thoughts and desires of a fallen human soul. Apollinaris' pupil and fellow fighter against Arianism, Gregory of Nazianzus (330–390), felt forced to oppose him. He saw that it was vital that Christ be fully human, otherwise he could not have penetrated the whole of human nature: 'What he has not assumed, he has not saved.'

The Antiochene School emphasized the reality of the human being, Jesus, and his willing submission to the divine Christ. It was important to distinguish between the human and the divine in Jesus Christ. The man Jesus had to assent to the union through a moral choice. A proponent of this tendency was

Nestorius, whose followers however went so far that the humanity and divinity started to seem quite separate. A great point of debate with Nestorius was the question whether it could be right to call Mary *Theotokos*, the God bearer. Nestorius affirmed that it could only be proper to call her *Christokos*, the Christ-bearer, that is, the bearer of the one who was to be united with God.

The climax of the quest to understand the person of Jesus Christ came at the fourth Council of the Church at Chalcedon in 451. The Definition of Chalcedon is a great dialectic, a dynamic movement between extremes.[9] It affirms the unity of Jesus Christ 'one and the same Son' and moves through a series of four concepts that are applied in turn to his divinity and his humanity. He is 'perfect in Godhead ... perfect in manhood,' 'truly God and truly man'; 'of one substance with the Father as touching the Godhead ... with us as touching the manhood.' The Definition then moves between the opposites of unity and distinction. Jesus Christ 'is known in two natures, without mixture, without change, without separation and without division.' The two natures contribute to forming 'one single person and one subsistence, not parted or divided into two persons, but one and the same Son, and only begotten, God the Word, the Lord Jesus Christ .'

The paradoxical clauses of this formula are very abstract, but they could never be described as static. The formulation of Chalcedon suggests in its very paradoxical language the dynamic of the Incarnation. In its 'in-between,' it brings to expression the weaving and working together of two different spheres.

Historically, Chalcedon was a limited success. Although it remains the touchstone of orthodoxy in the churches of the mainstream in both East and West, the hope that it would unite the different strands of Christian thinking was to be disappointed. To this day, there are groupings of Christians who hold to the different extremes: Monophysites who emphasize the oneness of divine and human in Jesus Christ; and Nestorians who see the importance of the distinctness of the two natures.

In the broad stream of orthodox Christian theology, the subject of the Incarnation did not receive much attention until the

Reformation; and even in this period which was so fertile for other areas, Christology did not take centre-stage. Only in the nineteenth century did Christians turn again to Chalcedon and its achievement — and then it was to reject it as an abstraction. The Incarnation came to be seen in symbolic terms, as figurative to express that in Jesus the 'God-consciousness' was maximally developed.

Son of Man

> What are the roots that clutch, what branches grow
> Out of this stony rubbish? Son of man,
> You cannot say, or guess, for you know only
> A heap of broken images, where the sun beats,
> And the dead tree gives not shelter, the cricket no relief,
> And the dry stone no sound of water.
> (Eliot 1986, p. 63)

'Son of Man' was a way of saying 'I' in Aramaic. In the book of Daniel, it is the title of a representative of humanity's future. Saint John used the same language in his Apocalypse. Ezekiel is called 'Son of Man' by Yahweh when he has to prophesy.

Christ refers to the Son of Man in the third person. The grammar that strains to bear all this meaning echoes Yahweh when he tells Moses to tell the Israelites: 'I am who I am has sent me.' Here, grammar simply explodes — either he should say: 'He who says 'I am who I am' has sent me,' or: 'I have sent myself.' It seems that in speaking of Yahweh, the third person, which distances me from what I am referring to, is not possible. We are used to speaking to God as 'you.' Here we learn that we can only really speak of him as 'I.' When Christ speaks of himself, the title 'Son of Man' expresses that the true 'I' of humanity is its future which is hidden in Christ, for in the image of a 'son' is contained the idea that humanity will give birth to something new. Christians needed twenty centuries before they could begin to understand this revelation, the revelation of the spirit through and in the human 'I.'

One of the prophets of this revelation was the English poet Gerard Manley Hopkins (1844–89). His life was one of failure and struggle; he was ostracized by his family and friends. Born an Anglican, he became a Jesuit out of a longing for true spiritual experience in worship. His superiors did not understand him and his teaching career was a disaster. His superiors rejected his poetry, and he was forbidden to write more, because, they said, it fostered vanity. He did finally destroy his copies of his poems, and they were only preserved to be published posthumously because his friend, Robert Bridges, disobeyed Hopkins' express wish that he destroy the copies Hopkins had sent him.

In the poem, 'That Nature is a Heraclitean Fire and of the Comfort of the Resurrection,' Hopkins indicates the depths of depression and desolation he had plumbed:

> ... Man, how fast his firedint, his mark on mind, is gone!
> Both are in an unfathomable, all is in an enormous dark
> Drowned. O pity and indignation! Manshape, that shone
> Sheer off, disseveral, a star, death blots black out; nor mark
> Is any of him at all so stark
> But vastness blurs and time beats level.

Then the mood is transformed in a turning that echoes the Psalmist whose words were quoted above:

> Enough! the Resurrection,
> A heart's-clarion! Away grief's gasping, joyless days,
>   dejection.
>   Across my foundering deck shone
> A beacon, an eternal beam. Flesh fade, and mortal trash
> Fall to the residuary worm; world's wildfire, leave but ash:
>   In a flash, at a trumpet crash,
> I am all at once what Christ is, since he was what I am, and
> This Jack, joke, poor potsherd, patch, matchwood, immortal
>   diamond,
>   Is immortal diamond.
>   (Hopkins 1970, pp. 105f)

In the depths of despair, Hopkins realizes that the Resurrection fulfils his humanity. 'I am all at once what he is, since he was what I am ...' This is the mystery of the Son of Man. When I am truly myself, he is at work as my 'I' within me.

The theology of the Son of Man starts from the personal and shows how living a human destiny, with its sufferings and moments of glory, reveals the living Christ. Dogmatic definitions of the person of Christ fall away. Instead, this theology describes the gesture of the seeking human being who strives towards that space between God and man, between heaven and earth, where Jesus Christ is at home.

... you are still asleep ...

It is I, I,
I lay between you, I was
Open, was
audible, ticked at you, your breathing
obeyed, it is
I still, but then
you are asleep.

Christ explodes the limitations of our humanity. He shows how hollow our idea of the good life is — and how it closes us off to the essence of our humanity, which is the essence of his humanity too. To promise human beings Batman — even in his guise as Christ — desecrates the memory of those for whom he did *not* come. Childish images of Christ the conqueror are an escape. The scandalous Wounded Healer has a far greater promise. He unites with that part of us which itself has the power to save, to redeem. This is the apocalyptic 'I,' which shines out in the darkness and pain of the modern world. After the needle's eye of modernity, which stripped us of the old images of the divine, we enter a new world that begins to fill, not with a cut and dried definition, but the description of a gesture, a movement infinitely tender and precious, a movement from heaven to earth, from God to Man — 'I am what he is, for he was what I am.'

> Years, years, a finger
> feels down and up, feels
> around:
> seems, palpable, here
> it is split wide open, here
> it grew together again — who
> covered it up?
> (Celan 1980, p. 60)

He weaves between heaven and earth, opening and closing to both realities like a heart, filling our heart. Of one substance with God — of one substance with us, says the Definition of Chalcedon. That is to say, the very fact of the Incarnation is an alchemical union through a weaving dynamic of what had been separate since the original unity was broken.

As in the earliest church, it is through the liturgy that we experience what we can only grope to explain. In the Act of Consecration of Man in Passiontide, we feel the heart growing empty; in Holy Week, the empty space is filled with a purifying flame. At Easter, the grave of the earthly body is 'empty'; the 'heart is full.' Celan reveals that Jesus Christ's heartbeat 'ticks at us.' Its rhythm becomes our rhythm. Our breathing is taken into his cosmic breath. The superheroes are a disturbing dream, a deceitful nightmare. True salvation — the new union between heaven and earth — is made possible by the joining of the two natures. Divinity and humanity are melded together and from then on can grow together. And in tune with the whole of creation, this happens not through coercion or by the magical overthrow of the conditions of our earthly existence, but through a sacrifice and a wound. The icon of this costly love draws us to make it real every day.

5. The Holy Spirit

We sit together trying to take a difficult decision for our community. We have to let go of an old idea of how things should develop, and make space for new ideas. Everyone is given space to speak about their dream. We leave two days' time and meet again. How will we arrive at a consensus, starting from such varied standpoints? The second meeting begins with one of the strongest opponents from the previous meeting speaking of her realization that her dream was just that: a dream that fitted her own longings. The mood of the meeting is transformed. The witness of one person to her process of offering up her cherished standpoint acts like alchemy. The spirit that unites us has spoken to us, and a true meeting has taken place; we have grown together as a community. Now, the community can decide what to do and the decision is carried by everyone.

It is hard to think about the Holy Spirit. The images of Father and Son are drawn from the most intimate realm of our human experience. Everyone had parents; everyone has been a child. Even traumatic childhoods prepare us to think of God as Father; our knowledge of what we lacked informs us what a father could or should be. Could we have such a relationship with something impersonal, with spirit?

This elusive name reflects the Spirit's reticent being. When we call upon the Spirit to 'enlighten' us in the Act of Consecration of Man, we gain an insight into this being. We can only see the world because it is illumined by light, but we are not aware of the light itself. When we see a beautiful landscape, we don't say: How wonderfully the light shines on the trees, the mountains and valleys! We rejoice in the sight, without thinking of the medium that makes it possible.

We are equally unaware of the qualities of soul which we need if we are to see, both inwardly and outwardly. We need to pay attention, to be interested; we need to reflect on the impressions we have. All of these qualities allow the world to become present to us. Again, we don't say: my attention is allowing me to see that you are there; our interest is making this a deep conversation. The Holy Spirit is the giver of light, both exterior and interior. Reflecting on him means reflecting on reflection itself — not something that comes easily! The prayer spoken in the Act of Consecration when there is no particular festival celebration subtly draws our attention to the Spirit as the unnoticed medium of our experience of God, which is itself God. Rather than just making statements about Father and Son, the first two parts of the prayer begin by telling us that it is our *consciousness* of our humanity that allows us to experience the Father; through *awareness* of Christ 'in our humanity' we experience the Son. The Spirit as the *medium* of our experience of both Father and Son is our consciousness, awareness. In the third part we do not hear statements, but a prayer that the Holy Spirit *may* be the light of our consciousness.

Rudolf Steiner gives us more background for understanding this in his descriptions of the experience of the Trinity.[10] He tells us that the experience of the Father lies *beneath* the level of the unconscious. This statement seems to be a contradiction: surely experience, if it is experience, has to be conscious. However, if we ask what is the most fundamental quality of the Father, we might think of the Ground of Existence. This is always with us; normally we only think about it when it seems to be taken away, in an earthquake, or when we suffer trauma, for example. The moment in every day life that brings us closest to experiencing it is when we surrender ourselves to sleep. It is astonishing that we do this seemingly as a matter of course. After all, we spend our days trying to keep ourselves together, safeguarding the integrity of body and soul. If someone offers to hypnotize us or take us out of ourselves we are rightly suspicious. But come the evening we gladly lie down and prepare to let go. In falling asleep we show our greatest faith in God as the ground of all being; we leave our body behind, trusting that there will be a body there, and there will be a world for us to live in, when we awake the next day.

This faith is the fruit of the kind of experience that Steiner means: in the moment of letting go, we are not consciously aware of our experience of the Father, the Ground of all Being. Nevertheless, we could never fall asleep if we did not have the faith that rests on this experience that lies deeper than any conscious awareness.

In relation to the experience of Christ, Steiner says that it resides *in* the unconscious. The Trinity prayer tells us that we experience Christ *in* our humanity, which leads us to the experience of God the Son. If the Father is the Ground that we experience when we are falling asleep or dying, the final deposit of being into whose hands we entrust ourselves, where do we experience the Son? He is the one who wrests new life from every death. We saw above the moment of transformation when the Psalmist finds the certainty he needs to proclaim the Messiah. The power that gives him his certainty and the content of the message are in fact one. The power of his inner resurrection gives him strength to proclaim that there will be a resurrection in the world to come. Such moments of certainty can occur in every human biography.

We are quarrelling seemingly without end. No matter what words I use, you do not hear what I am trying to say. And later I see that the real problem is that the words I'm trying so hard to get you to hear are drowning out the words you're saying to me — words that I've been ignoring for the last two years. The lovely celebration we planned for this evening is ruined. In the end you leave, and only our friend stays with me. She doesn't try to sort me out — she knows my words would drown her out too. She just keeps saying: I don't think you're really hearing what she's trying to say to you! I don't know what it might be that I'm not hearing. But in the end I decide to go and try. I come into the room. The tear in the fabric that unites us is palpable. I am full of fear. I open my mouth to speak — I have no idea what I'm going to say. To my amazement words start to come out, in a different tone of voice. The tear has been repaired. There are many more things to talk about, but the most important thing has been done. New life has been born. In opening my mouth, in finding new

> *breath, I found new words — I found the Word, who is there*
> *in every new beginning.*

Awareness — unconscious awareness, if we can grasp that — of the power of resurrection makes it possible to open our mouths, to find the first word to say. It is quite a different process to reflect on this, to understand who it is who is at work in me when I manage to do this. It was hard even for Christ's disciples to understand that he was the Messiah, the bringer of new life. Only when the Holy Spirit came at Whitsun were they able fully to grasp it. Remarkably, in the great sermon that Peter holds (see Acts, Chapter 2), the Spirit does not take centre stage, in spite of his dramatic arrival in the tongues of flame. His coming is only mentioned as evidence that the prophecies have been fulfilled. And yet Holy Spirit fills the sermon and makes understanding possible, just as those listening could only see because the sun had risen that morning. The audience already had all the information concerning Jesus; some of them had evidently witnessed events in his life and death. It is the gift of the Spirit that makes it possible for them to understand what until now has been dim experience, or has even been misunderstood. However, even now the message is not forced upon them. A very special kind of attention is needed, along with a willingness to throw overboard all preconceived ideas. To those who are not ready to do this, the whole thing seems to be the ravings of a drunken rabble. Just as we have to open our eyes to experience the world, the gift of the light, we need to open our inner eyes to the Spirit.

All of this describes what the Spirit *does* — his *function*. But this is of course at the same time a revelation of what the Spirit *is*. We saw above Augustine's beautiful image of Trinity: the Father as lover, the Son as beloved, and the Spirit as the love that unites them. Both Father and Son are persons in this image. The Spirit is an activity — the deed of love. This activity brings about a perfect interpenetration.

Through love, two partners are drawn together in a new unity; when we love, our beloved lives within us, and we in her or him. What he or she feels is our own feeling; our lover's joys and sorrows are our own. When human beings open their inner eyes and allow the Spirit to work, they are drawn into the love that unites the Godhead. When Christ promises to send the Holy Spirit he says to them: 'On that day you will realize that I am in my Father, and you are in me, and I am in you' (John 14:20, NIV). Hence the Trinity Epistle talks about the *healing* Spirit. All disease, all illness ultimately stems from our being separate from our origin. The deepest healing means to be reunited with our source in God.

Grasping the Spirit

It took the longest for Christians to understand the Spirit — if we ever really have. Throughout the disputes of the fourth century, the place of the Holy Spirit in the Trinity was a kind of afterthought. Only gradually did the insight grow up that the third person of the Trinity must also be a part of Godhead, and not a separate or lesser entity. Even in the reworking of the Nicene Creed that was undertaken in Constantinople in 381, the divinity of the Spirit is really only implied by the fact that he is to be worshipped and glorified like Father and Son.

The next question that arose concerning the Spirit was the question of his 'procession.' Does he 'proceed' only from the Father, as the original version of the Creed of 381 implies, or does he proceed from both the Father and the Son? This was the so-called *filioque* dispute (in Latin *filioque* means 'and from the Son'). This was one of the theological issues that led to the schism or divide between the Eastern, Orthodox churches and the Roman Catholic church. The Orthodox churches held to the original wording of the Creed, whereas the *filioque* was accepted in the Latin West. Orthodox scholars rightly point out that the Western teaching on the Spirit has been abused by the church, which began to see itself as the only dispenser of the Holy Spirit in Christ's name. Orthodoxy has always been more open to the working of the Spirit in other religions and in the mystics. However, the deeper meaning of the *filioque* is the insight that the sending of the Holy Spirit at Whitsun is the beginning of a second creation. Through the Holy Spirit, Christ begins the work of gathering the shattered and splinted shards of the first creation into the new union — into community. This is not just a restoration of the old creation. The sending of the Holy Spirit through Christ takes us into the heart of the Advent mystery that God's becoming and our becoming as human beings are intertwined.

Human and holy

The working of the Holy Spirit allows God to come alive within the human spirit. What is the connection between these two spirits, one divine and one human? The Bible often speaks of the 'spirit' of human beings. For Saint Paul, this is part of a worked-out picture of the human being, who consists of body, soul and spirit. And of course the image which is the Spirit's name in Greek and Hebrew — wind or breath — expresses the fact that spirit can spread into many places whilst maintaining its connection to the one Spirit, the great breath of the world.

The Bible also speaks of human beings who are 'holy.' In the New Testament, these are the ones who have dedicated themselves to Christ — the 'saints.' It was only later that this word came to be used particularly and then exclusively of those who had died for their dedication. A modern translation might echo the title of our Communion Service, and render it 'those who have experienced the consecration of their humanity.' Perhaps every human being who has turned in inner dedication to the world of spirit has or, in some way, is, Holy Spirit.

We have seen how Christ approaches us as the archetype of our future becoming — as Son of Man. The working of the Holy Spirit allows us to realize this archetype within ourselves — to draw it into ourselves — just as it draws us towards it. The image of the many different flames into which the Spirit divides at Whitsun means that there is nothing mechanical or coercive about our becoming one with Christ. Each 'immortal diamond' is utterly individual and unique.

In the traditional division of roles amongst the persons of the Trinity, the Father is Creator and Sustainer; the Son is Redeemer, and the Holy Spirit is the Sanctifier. What does this mean? Literally it means he makes us saints, he consecrates our humanity. What happens when we forget ourselves in prayer or worship, or in performance or action where we go beyond our-selves, does not come from us. We know that something greater is at work in us, through us. Nevertheless, it would not have happened if we had not got up and gone to the church, or got out of bed and folded our hands and prayed. Our human spirit and Holy Spirit cooperate for us to be consecrated.

Saint Patrick *(ca.* 390 – *ca.* 461) describes two experiences of this cooperation:

> And another night — God knows, I do not, whether within me or beside me — words ... which I heard and could not understand, except at the end of the speech it was represented thus: 'He who gave his life for you, he it is who speaks within you.' And thus I awoke, joyful.
>
> And on a second occasion I saw Him praying within me, and I was as it were, inside my own body, and I heard Him above me — that is, above my inner self. He was praying powerfully with sighs. And in the course of this I was astonished and wondering, and I pondered who it could be who was praying within me. But at the end of the prayer it was revealed to me that it was the Spirit. And so I awoke and remembered the Apostle's words: 'Likewise the Spirit helps us in our weakness; for we know not how to pray as we ought. But the Spirit Himself intercedes for us with sighs too deep for utter-ance.'
>
> (*Confession*, Book 7, 24–45)

There is a whole realm of experience for which we lack the lan-guage. Every speaker, every artist, every workman or teacher, every counsellor, and also everyone who simply prays, knows moments when something speaks through us that is greater than we ourselves. Yet it is not possession. If we said 'it had nothing to do with me,' we would feel untruthful. If we said 'I did it' we would be in danger of hubris. Our very struggling for words is a clue that we are groping towards the being of the Spirit, the God of interpenetration — of representation — of mutual indwelling of beings.

Koinonia

Paul often speaks of the *koinonia* of the Holy Spirit. *Koinonia* is usually translated as 'fellowship' or 'communion.' It comes from an ancient Greek word meaning partner, sharer or joint owner. It is a community born of both partners having a share in something held in common. What is the *koinonia* of the Holy Spirit? As the bond of love in the Trinity, he is the community of life of the Godhead. As the one who lets the knowledge of God shine in our consciousness, he extends that community of life to us. In the image of the tongues of fire at Whitsun we see the fulfilment of the movement from unity to multiplicity. This multiplicity though is no multitude, no rabble. It is community in the making. Inspired by the Spirit of *koinonia*, the apostles are ready to draw those who were lost in their separateness into a new *koinonia* that celebrates new life.

'See how these Christians love one another!' Tertullian (*ca.* 160–*ca.* 220) reports as the reaction of educated pagans, dismayed by the astonishingly rapid growth of the church. The factors behind that growth have been puzzled over for many centuries. Certain factors that contributed are clear: the openness to women and slaves, and the good works the Christians did for each other — in other words, the *koinonia* of the Spirit that animated the church — were important.

Holy Spirit is at work in all human beings who raise their gaze to the mysteries of God. Their individual human spirits become part of the 'communion of saints' — the *koinonia* of those who have experienced the consecration of their humanity. Every Christian creed has moved from the oneness of God and creation and the salvation through Christ to the Holy Spirit and his *koinonia*, the new unity which is the beginning of a new creation in which all the disparate parts will be gathered into a great wholeness once more. Christ, speaking in the Holy Spirit in the High Priestly Prayer, says: 'I in them and you in me. May they be brought to complete unity to let the world know that you sent me and have loved them even as you have loved me' (John 17:23, NIV).

The Spirit of evolution

The work of the Spirit goes far beyond 'religious' activities. Spirit is at work in the processes of evolution and becoming. In fact if we take in the idea that Holy Spirit is relationship, dynamic, then we find traces everywhere in the world. It is a fact that popular awareness of science always lags behind the pioneers of science. Many scientific lay-people today are under the impression that we have to choose between a religious picture of the world, where the ultimate reality is relationship, love and consciousness; or a materialistic one, where atoms bang up against each other by chance and nature is 'red in tooth and claw.' Whilst it is true that the materialistic explanation of the universe gives chance a great role in the processes of evolution, what evolves is not random in itself. If we have the idea of Holy Spirit as relationship and dynamic, then the descriptions of the relationships of forces at the subatomic level, and of the relationships of symbiosis within organisms and of ecosystems between them become a revelation of Spirit at work.

The German idealist philosopher Hegel (1770–1831) saw that through the Holy Spirit, Creation awakens to itself, to its own origin. In the idea of 'sanctification' lies something far deeper than the idea of becoming saintly: the Holy Spirit draws creation towards its fulfilment. He is supremely the Spirit of evolution that draws creatures along their path towards personhood, choice and creative, self-bestowing love.[11] Spirit is both outside and within the creatures as they move towards their great aim. This is the truth expressed in the Advent Epistle. God's becoming continues through our becoming. There is a paradox here, one which Hegel perhaps failed to grasp. He saw in Father, Son and Spirit 'moments' of the actualization of God's being. Holy Spirit only comes into being when human beings develop self-reflective thought, and mirror the Creator back to himself. But if God is wholly dependent on human development, is he really God? What of the Spirit that brooded on the waters at Creation? Nevertheless, Hegel perceived a vital part of the reality of God — a part which makes us aware of our huge responsibility, but also of the immense help that is available to us.

Every thought we think, every deed we do can be the Spirit working if it is open to the Spirit.

In this way, we can see the Act of Consecration as the archetypal human activity. Although its prayers are addressed almost exclusively to God the Father and the Son, we can know that in praying them we both speak and hear Holy Spirit. He is the current of communication that flows from the congregation through the celebrant to the divine world, and that allows the human community to open itself for the flow of life of the holy Trinity. The Act of Consecration is a celebration of *koinonia*. The community of life of the congregation is embodied in the common offering that flows together in the cup. Our community of life with Christ is strengthened when our offering is taken into Christ's offering, and his life flows into and permeates our life. And when the bread and the wine are finally lifted up to become Christ's body and blood, we call upon the Spirit with words that are his own. For his being is the flow from heaven to earth, from earth to heaven; his work is the indwelling, interpenetrating, intermingling of *koinonia*. We ask that his grace may be at work, flowing from heaven, meeting and mingling with the offering that rises from the earth — from his working within us.

The early church's insights on the Spirit remained incomplete and elusive. Particularly the link between the human and the Holy Spirit grew increasingly dim, until the moment in the Council of Constantinople in 869 when it was denied that human beings were possessed of a spirit as an autonomous entity, but rather that they possessed souls with spiritual attributes.[12] This tragic decision — the counterpart to the banishing of the Trinity to a realm so far distant from our experience that the world became empty of Spirit — sets the stage for the development of the modern picture of man, which goes a step further and denies even an independent reality of the soul. One fundamental task of The Christian Community is to explore what it can mean to create communities of human beings that do not deny their spiritual integrity but build on it.

6. Evil Calls for its Redemption

In the fourth chapter of the Book of Revelation, we are shown a vision of heaven before the beginning of time. God sits upon his throne surrounded by a sea of glass. There is movement, but the image of the sea of glass makes it seem as if that movement is frozen. Glory radiates out from the throne; it is received and mirrored back again. At the beginning of the fifth chapter, the tragic side of this state is revealed. The book of life is brought in. No-one can open it. The image of the book represents something quite different from what went before. The circulation of glory is an ever-repeating cycle. A book represents a narrative with a beginning, a middle and an end. The fact that it cannot be opened shows how difficult the transition from a world of pure being to a world of becoming is. God as the eternal ground of all being cannot also be the principle of becoming.

The problem is solved by the mysterious figure of the lamb which looks as if it had been sacrificed. Only he can open the book and resolve the dilemma. From this moment on, the whole drama of creation unfolds as the seals are opened one by one and the events of the Book of Revelation begin.

We might ask at this point where we are in the story. Surely the sacrifice of the lamb is an image for the Crucifixion — something that happened long after the creation of the world. The Book of Revelation shows us that what happened on Golgotha was itself an echo of the sacrifice that underlies all creation. Plato tells of the world soul being stretched out in creation on the dimensions of time and space as if on a cross.[13]

The image of the sacrificial lamb has yet more layers to reveal. How has the lamb been sacrificed? A destructive power must be at work.

One of the most stirring moments in the narrative of the

Passion comes when Christ predicts his betrayal. He speaks to Judas: 'What you have to do, do it!' It almost seems that he gives Judas a commission to fulfil his part in the drama of redemption and new creation. Does the lamb's sacrifice come about through the working of powers opposed to things remaining as they are? And are they given a commission? The origin of the adversary forces is not explained in the pictures of the Book of Revelation, just as the origin of the serpent in the Garden of Eden is not explained; nor indeed is the riddle of Judas explained in the New Testament. We are invited into a deep mystery, for it seems that the adversary forces actually act to further the course of evolution. Without the sacrifice of the lamb — without there being a principle that can check and counter the unity of being — there can be no becoming, differentiation, or development.

Life-experience teaches us that it is not the times when everything is going well that make us grow and learn, but those when we are struggling with adversity. It is hard for us to imagine that what can seem like a very personal and everyday principle is in fact a cosmic one. What we experience is that there is a natural line of our development which, left unchecked, would not bring us to maturity. We need to struggle with something that counters our development.

If we try to summarize the pitfalls into which we fall, we find that they can be put into two groups: those that take us away from the earth, and those that tie us too closely to the earth. Knowing that there are two tendencies can be a great help. Instead of the binary situation, where we have to choose between good and evil, black or white, right or wrong, we see that there is always a dynamic at work. Doing 'good' doesn't mean deciding on one course and staying there — it means accepting that we are on a journey. We shall look at this more closely in the second part of this book.

This is why the good is never the simple opposite of the bad. For example, there is a tendency towards extravagance, which we could see on the earth-denying side of things. Its opposite is miserliness — too great a concentration on earthly possessions. If I discover that I am too extravagant, it would be bad advice to tell me to become a miser; instead, I need to find the middle, where I am conscious of the cost of things, but use my resources generously to enable what needs to come about. We can see the same in relation to many pairings of vices: what is the opposite of foolhardiness, an attitude that forgets the reality of earthly danger? Would it be cowardice? The quality of the middle is courage. What is the opposite of hyperactivity? Lethargy? The middle would be a balanced approach to life.

'Evil evil'

There is however another quality of the working of the adversaries that seems to go beyond this. This is what we might think of as really evil. This is what is unleashed in exceptional circumstances which seems to attack the very core of the human being and leave no space for a compensating movement back into the wholeness of the middle. It is well summed up in these words of Dostoevsky, from *The Brothers Karamazov:*

> In every man, of course, a demon lies hidden — the demon of rage, the demon of lustful heat at the screams of the tortured victim, the demon of lawlessness let off the chain.
> (Dostoevsky 2002, p. 623)

It is this evil that is unleashed by the strange circumstances of national or ethnic psychosis that have marked the history of the twentieth and twenty-first centuries.

In this kind of evil we can often recognize both of the other kinds working together and indeed enhancing each other. Rudolf Steiner recognizes these forces of evil as being more than just tendencies within the human being. They are beings, for whom he uses names drawn from the religious heritage of humanity. Lucifer is the being that would draw us away from the earth, making us vain and proud. Ahriman is the being who would reduce us to mere earthly beings and crush us under the weight of the earth. A third being, about which Rudolf Steiner speaks relatively little, manifests only in our time: the being called Sorat, who works through Lucifer and Ahriman to achieve a level of evil hitherto unknown.

It is a special quality of our age that for the first time, many human beings have faced the fact that there is evil within them — what Steiner called the furnace of destruction in every human being. There have been experiments — recently dramatized in the film, *The Wave* — that show how easily people can give way to the suggestion that doing destructive things is right. The new quality of evil that is projected so terrifyingly on to the stage of world-history, magnified in its possibilities by technology, has made human beings wake up to the task of acknowledging evil within themselves — and of becoming explorers of their inner world.

Whilst we can almost feel grateful for the work of the adversaries that give us the chance to develop the forces of our middle, and that allow the world to develop on its course, there is something so corrosive about the third kind of evil that we may feel almost offended by any attempt too neatly to fit it into a great scheme of things. If we feel this we are in good company. Philosophers through the ages have grappled with the problem of reconciling a good God with the bad things that happen in the world. The problem was first summed up by Epicurus, the Greek philosopher of the third century BC. Either God could prevent evil and he chooses not to, in which case he is a monster; or he would like to prevent it but cannot, in which case he is not God, if we understand God to mean the most powerful being that exists.

We have already seen that the old idea of God sitting outside the universe and showering good things on those who obey him, and punishing those who do not, is no longer tenable today. We have seen God much more within the processes of evolution. We could of course solve the problem of the existence of destructive evil with the completely logical thought that there is indeed a limit on God's power, if we take power to mean doing things that are impossible, or logically incoherent. The philosophers love the example of the triangle. Can God make a triangle with four sides? Surely not — not unless we change the meaning of the word triangle. Similarly it is argued that the idea of a created world without evil, or without quite so much evil, is as nonsensical as the four-sided triangle. But such logical reflections rarely satisfy our need to understand on a deeper level.

A simple reflection on prayer can show us that we need this deeper understanding. If I pray that bad things might not happen to someone I love, or indeed to the world, I am convinced that God has the power to prevent these things. If I really believe that God is just another name for the blind process of development, or that he is powerless to change anything in the world, I wouldn't pray to him. But if he has the power to prevent the things that touch me, could he not have prevented the terrible evils of genocide in the last decades? Am I to understand somehow that the terrible deaths in the concentration camps — the mass rapes, the murders and torture that still happen today — that all this is somehow justified, that it is part of God's plan?

Here I believe that it is important to learn from people who feel no obligation to hold on to a framework of meaning. Atheists are sometimes far more honest than religious people in articulating the reality of evil and suffering, and in this way they are more compassionate. We may know from our own experience that it does not help if our friends come too soon with their helpful insights about how what has befallen us is the outworking of our destiny, and will in fact turn out to be a blessing. It is a failure of compassion that often stems from an unwillingness to face the reality of the desolation we can all feel in the face of suffering and evil.

Rebellion and redemption

Dostoevsky's Ivan Karamazov explains to his brother Alyosha that he has decided to commit suicide, because he wants to reject God's plan for the world, and suicide is the only way of 'returning his entry-ticket.' This is because he has experienced the cruelty of human beings to each other, and been told that it is all in God's plan for the earth. He brings examples of unspeakable cruelty to children, which Dostoevsky in fact took from newspaper reports of the day. One was about babies being thrown out of windows on to the bayonets of soldiers waiting below. Another concerned a little girl who had been found having been locked up by her parents in a shed, starving and covered in her own excrement. In another, a peasant child had

thrown a stone at a hunting dog and lamed it, and his parents
were forced to watch whilst he was stripped naked and hunted
down by the pack, which then tore him to pieces. Ivan explains
his case against God:

> 'Do you understand that, friend and brother, you pious
> and humble novice? Do you understand why this infamy
> must be and is permitted? Without it, I am told, man
> could not have existed on earth, for he could not have
> known good and evil. Why should he know that diaboli-
> cal good and evil when it costs so much? ... I say nothing
> of the sufferings of grown-up people, they have eaten the
> apple, damn them, and the devil take them all! But these
> little ones! I am making you suffer, Alyosha, you are not
> yourself. I'll leave off if you like.'
>   'Never mind. I want to suffer too,' muttered Alyosha.
> ...
>   'Tell me yourself, I challenge your answer. Imagine
> that you are creating a fabric of human destiny with the
> object of making men happy in the end, giving them
> peace and rest at last, but that it was essential and
> inevitable to torture to death only one tiny creature —
> that baby beating its breast with its fist, for instance —
> and to found that edifice on its unavenged tears, would
> you consent to be the architect on those conditions? Tell
> me, and tell the truth.' 'No, I wouldn't consent,' said
> Alyosha softly.
>   [Alyosha says] 'You said just now, is there a being in
> the whole world who would have the right to forgive
> and could forgive? But there is a Being and He can for-
> give everything, all and for all, because He gave His
> innocent blood for all and everything. You have forgotten
> Him, and on Him is built the edifice, and it is to Him
> they cry aloud, "Thou art just, O Lord, for Thy ways are
> revealed!"'
>   (Dostoevsky 2002, pp. 624–36)

Alyosha's answer could sound like a pious platitude. How easy
to wheel on Christ as the answer to every problem! The course

he takes as the novel unfolds shows that he takes it far more seriously than this. He decides to suffer the punishment for the murder of his father, of which he is innocent, believing that by taking on himself undeserved suffering he will add to the sum of the forces of redemption in the world.

And now we can return to the image of the little child hanging on the gallows in Auschwitz, and Elie Wiesel hearing the question, 'Where is merciful God?' His answer has a dimension far deeper than even he realized, when he said: 'Hanging from this gallows.' For in the centre of Christianity is the experience that God is there, hanging on the gallows — that he is in every experience of evil, every experience of loss and desolation that human beings have to go through. He is the wounded healer — the one whose mysterious power to save us comes not from his strength but his weakness.

How dare I say such a thing, I, a Christian who have never experienced the radical evil that Wiesel, a Jew, was witnessing at that moment? I have asked myself this over and over again, the most intensely perhaps when I was standing on the parade ground between the barracks of the first camp at Auschwitz. I have always wondered whether it is right to allow myself to think that I might know something about these questions when my faith has never been tested in such extreme circumstances. Am I like one of those glib friends that rush to tell us that there is meaning in our pain?

Strangely, when I stood by the gallows in Auschwitz, and when I walked up the Jew-ramp to the crematoria at the top of the second camp, Auschwitz-Birkenau, I did not feel crushed by the realization of evil, although seeing the steps the millions walked down on their way into the gas-chambers gave me a shock like being kicked in the stomach. I wondered why I didn't feel shaken or overwhelmed; then I realized that this reality has been part of my world for as long as I could remember. The new and shocking realization was that I was the future of those millions. Here I was, standing here and thinking of them, who had probably so longed that someone would stand and think of them. It struck me that whilst it was not in my power to change the past, nor to make it 'all right,' it was in my power to live to the best of my strength in memory of them, and in the awareness of the evil that lives inside each one of us; to work to redeem what evil I can in myself, and to cultivate the right attitude to evil wherever I find it, in myself and others — to speak up and condemn the evil, but to be forgiving of the one who does it; to be aware that the tendency towards evil is written into the fabric of the universe, and that I can do something, if only a very little, to work for its redemption.

*   *   *

How does God, who is apart from space and time, create the world of space and time, get involved in the fabric of being? It is through emptying himself, through being stretched out — crucified — on the dimensions of space and time. The Book of Revelation adds to this image the sacrificial element — only the sacrificial lamb can open the book of becoming. How does God bring about the new creation, the salvation of all, and the redemption of all the pain and sorrow of the earth? By his deed of sacrifice, joining us in the midst of radical evil and submitting to its worst effects.

None of this is an answer to the intellectual argument that accuses God for making a world full of suffering, or rejects his existence because of this world. Like Alyosha Karamazov, when we recognize this truth we have no option but to act. His brother's problem is not really an argument but an objection of taste. He doesn't wish to be part of the world which is made in this way. Alyosha doesn't try to defeat him with an intellectual proof. There is no intellectual answer to the mystery of evil, the consequence of our journey away from our original unity with the Spirit. We can only be true to our horror and shock in the face of it, and recognize the deed that transforms it with our own attempts to do a deed of transformation. 'I shall call out your name in the congregation … for thou hast done the deed!' says the Psalmist. The second part of this book is concerned with the community that witnesses to the deed.

Part 2: The New Community

We look at this Son and see an icon of the God who cannot be seen. We look at this Son and see God's original purpose in everything created.

For everything, absolutely everything, above and below, visible and invisible, rank after rank after rank of angels — everything was created through him and towards him.

He was there before any of it came into existence and he holds it all together right up to this moment.

And he is the head of the body, and his body is the great community of the communities of Christ.

He was supreme in the beginning and — leading the resurrection parade — he is supreme in the end. From beginning to end he's there, towering far above everything, everyone.

So spacious is he, so roomy, that everything of God finds its proper place in him without crowding.

Not only that, but all the broken and dislocated pieces of the universe — people and things, animals and atoms — get properly fixed and fit together in vibrant harmonies, all because of his death, his blood that poured down from the cross.

> (Saint Paul's Letter to the Colossians 1: 15–20. *The Message*, modified)

7. The Icon of the New Community

It could well be that the passage from Colossians quoted above was a hymn that was sung in the congregations Paul founded and visited. And if this is so, it may well have contained elements that went back to pre-Christian times. Inspiration never works in a vacuum — it draws on words, concepts, poetry that have existed before. The words of the hymn to Christ in Colossians could easily have been a Greek hymn to the divine *Logos* — until the point where it refers to the community of communities, the church. In a Stoic hymn to the *Logos*, the creator-spirit of the world, he would have been head of the body of the world. In Paul's version, he is the head of the *ekklesia*, the community of Christ.

This could seem like a huge narrowing-down — a universal concern has become the affair of one religious grouping, in Paul's day a tiny splinter group of the tiny Jewish religion. It could also seem like typical Christian arrogance — wanting to appropriate the Creator-God for their own party.

There is another possible interpretation. Could Paul be saying that wherever things are moving towards Christ, the divine *Logos*, that is *ekklesia* — the community called out of the world to a new orientation? This would be a truly cosmic Christianity — cosmic meaning here 'of the world,' from the Greek *kosmos*, meaning the world. Wherever the world is moving towards its fulfilment, its true destination, it is becoming the community of Christ.

It is a challenge to understand that the salvation of the whole of creation can come from one particular historic event, one particular human biography. This challenge starts with the story of the Jewish people who are told that their destiny will bring salvation to the whole world. In the legends of the Jews,

Abraham's decision to leave Mesopotamia is sparked off by the building of the Tower of Babel, the deed of a culture inspired by fear of the consequences of the separation which is clearly the lot of humanity: 'Come, let us build a city and a tower with its top reaching heaven, so that we may make ourselves a great name and not be scattered over the face of the earth!' (Genesis 11:4). The consequence is that the progressive spirits of evolution bring about a great confusion in language. From then on, human beings are divided. This is part of humanity's journey towards full incarnation in earthly existence. Our own experience teaches us this: to be incarnate means to be something particular, and therefore to be limited. We are a woman or a man, European or Asian, Christian or Jain. We can't be everything!

This backdrop helps us to understand the strange tension between particularity and universality that exists in the story of the Jewish people until today. The process of forming a particular folk with a connection to a particular spiritual being is the means by which Yahweh prepares for a future where a new, universal humanity will come to fulfilment. He promises that Abraham's descendants will mirror the stars in the heavens — on the one hand, an indication of their number, but more importantly, a symbol of their universality. He tells him that 'the nations of the world will be blessed in them' (Genesis 12:3). At the same time, the inauguration of the specific, Jewish bloodline is instituted through circumcision, and the principle of spiritual-physical descent starts with the rejection of the bloodline of Sara's Egyptian maid, Hagar, who bears Abraham's first son, Ishmael.

As the story of the Jewish people progresses, the double strands of the formation of a particular people and the development of its all-embracing task go hand in hand. We witness Jacob wrestling with the angel whose name is echoed in the Michaelmas epistle of the Act of Consecration — *Pni-el*, the countenance of God — and receiving the blessing and the name of his people: Israel, the one who wrestles with God. We witness a folk-spirit taking on his task. This is supremely a moment of folk-formation. But from this moment and its blessing flows the fulfilment of the promise made originally to Abraham — Jacob has twelve sons, whose tribes form an image of the twelve signs of the zodiac, the 'stars in the heavens' of the promise.

After the sojourn in Egypt, the loose federation of tribes becomes a people that receives its calling through Moses. It is to be a 'kingdom of priests, a holy people' (Exodus 19:6). Within a people in the ancient world, the priestly caste fulfilled the task of maintaining the connection with the god of the people. Within the community of peoples, the Jewish people is to take on a priestly role, connecting all the various peoples with the God of humanity. At the same, time, they are to be 'holy.' Holy in the ancient world meant simply separate. Something holy was removed from the normal world in order to be dedicated to a divine purpose. In giving the Jewish people the task of being 'a holy people,' Yahweh shows that the fulfilment of their universal task lies to begin with at least in a radical separation from the rest of humanity.

As the story goes on and the Jewish people enter the Holy Land, the tension between the universal mission of the Jews and their destiny as a folk grows. At times Yahweh appears to be a folk-god alongside those of the other peoples, guiding his people in battle and wreaking vengeance on their enemies; in the next moment he seems to be an icon of the Holy Trinity, connecting the people to the greatest aims of humanity.

In the Roman world, the Jews were known as fanatical nationalists, the one conquered nation that would not embrace the Roman emperor-cult. In the Roman Pantheon — the assembly of all the gods, to which the gods of every conquered people were added — we sense not a new oneness but a conquering uniformity. Soon after Jesus Christ lived and died, every local cult was supplemented by the cult of emperor-worship.

This was the spiritual background of the Incarnation of Christ into the Jewish people. We have seen in previous chapters the challenge of making the Incarnation real for ourselves. Can we imagine that in Jesus Christ, the Son of God, the Creator-Spirit whose body was once the sun, became a human being who lived in a particular time and place? Only by feeling this challenge — which theologians call the 'scandal of particularity' — do we appreciate the depth of the mystery of Christianity. This particular incarnation in the first century was the deepest, highest, most intense meeting of spirit and matter, when the soul of a human being united as closely with the divine Son as iron glowing in the fire, as Origen puts it.[14]

The union of ultimate reality with an earthly, limited being means that the Incarnation was the 'Ursacrament' — the archetype of every sacrament that followed. Every celebration of the Act of Consecration of Man asks us to make real for ourselves that Christ becomes present in the bread and wine that we feel on our lips and taste in our mouths.

The early Christians had an inkling of this combination of the universal and the particular. Justin the Martyr died for refusing to take part in the emperor-cult in 161. He taught that all reasonable human beings are gifted with the *Logos;* they possess a seed of the divine reason which was implanted in their breast when they were created. Human beings who lived out of this logos-seed were 'Christians before Christ.' We can take this thought further than Justin did, to realize that Christ is far more than can be contained in any religion, as a religion must be the product of a particular culture, language and time. The technical name for earthly things as windows on spiritual realities is *icon.* If we acknowledge that all such icons are limited, we can be touched by the reality towards which they point without needing to cling to their form. The church, then, has the task of being an icon, a window on the reality of Jesus Christ; it can never claim to 'have' the whole of him. Only the Incarnation of Jesus Christ has fully embodied ultimate reality in an earthly form. Through him, the possibility that earthly reality can become transparent for spiritual working has been opened — but all earthly forms are by their nature limited, particular.

After the fourth century, however, another tendency began to emerge in church history. The icon has a negative counterpart: the idol. An idol is no longer a window on the universal reality of the spirit, but it becomes a thing to be worshiped in itself. The tendency to idolatry — a danger inherent in every religion — was at work in the history of the church particularly from the fourth century on, when the church became an instrument of Roman state policy. The 'catholic' church — meaning simply the universal church — gradually became the Roman Catholic Church. Later, this principle went further, when churches were named after their founders: the Nestorian church, the Lutheran church.

It was a narrow-minded, idolatrous spirit that dominated the Christian communities of the Arabian peninsula in the seventh century, when the questing soul of the young Muhammad sought to find a way to bring the Arabian tribes to monotheism. It seems that the Arabs had been deemed to be unworthy of missionary efforts by either the Jewish or Christian faith, who saw them as inferior. The particular thought forms, language and symbols which Christians were used to, had become ends in themselves — idols. The church that was born in Paul's battle with those who clung to the particular forms of worshipping God given in the Old Testament, who had insisted that before a Galatian could be Christian he or she had to become Jewish, now insisted in its turn that, before an Arab could become Christian, he or she would have to become Greek.

The Christian Community

What of our task in The Christian Community? In its title it reverts to the usage of the early church: it is not the church of a particular nation, nor that of a particular teacher or leader. It acknowledges that the forms appropriate for worship are bound to time. It even looks to the time in a far-distant future when such worship — holy and therefore separate from the world — will not be necessary — when all human life will be imbued with spirit once more. In the meantime its task is to celebrate Christ's deed. We might distinguish two aspects of this. One is universal. We celebrate this in every Act of Consecration, but particularly on Easter Sunday, and in the weeks leading up to the Ascension. It is summed up in the words of the Creed: *Then he overcame death after three days.* This changed reality itself. We can call this aspect objective: it happened, whether or not anyone noticed or did anything about it.

The second aspect could be called subjective. This has to do with the appropriation of what Christ achieved. This is the aspect that shines out at Whitsun. The Apostles realize that it is not enough that Christ died and rose for human beings: human beings need to hear about it, and to live lives that embody the reality of the Resurrection.

The idolatrous tendency has often led human beings to think that this appropriation means accepting a particular teaching, or belonging to a particular church — and thus 'being good.' However, our experience of life tells us that neither holding particular things to be true, nor wearing a particular badge, guarantees that anyone lives the kind of life that Jesus lived, spreading the power that overcomes death. The Creed of The Christian Community is instructive on this point: *he will in time unite for the advancement of the world with those whom, through their bearing, he can wrest from the death of matter.* It is a question not of our intellectual convictions, but of our *bearing*, our deeds, whether Christ will be able to work through us.

Such a thought lay behind the phrase 'anonymous Christians' coined by the Catholic scholar, Karl Rahner (1904–84): Christ is at work far beyond the bounds of the church, just as he is not necessarily at work in all that the church does. Of course, adherents of other religions have responded by returning the compliment:

> And there are in fact Hindu philosophers who say that
> devout Christians are Advaita Vedantists at heart,
> because they have a real desire for the truth although
> they do not yet know what the truth is. They are anony-
> mous Hindus. And likewise there are Muslim theolo-
> gians who say that the devout Christian has Islam in his
> heart and is an anonymous Muslim. (Hick 2004)

The seeming absurdity of this brings John Hick to abandon all claims of ultimate revelation, including the Incarnation. With great sincerity he treads the path towards a positive relativism. If we see Christianity as just as one of the religions, we must do the same. There is however another possibility: that we grapple with the reality that Christ is greater than any of his churches, and greater indeed than the Christian religion itself. When we look back on the evil that has been done in the name of idolatrous religion, including that which bore the label 'Christian,' it is easy to understand the reaction against religion which has been a feature of the last two centuries, and which has reached a climax today. But to be aware of the dangers of doing something badly does not mean that we should not do it. Knowledge of the danger of idolatry can be a mirror to examine ourselves in. It can help us in our task of being an icon to the world of the new community, the new oneness between heaven and earth made possible by Christ.

The community of the second coming

When, in the years before the First World War, Rudolf Steiner started to speak about the Second Coming or *parousia*, Christ's becoming present to us in a new way, it must have seemed like something that could only be accepted on faith. In the meantime a literature has emerged which describes experiences that correspond very closely to Steiner's predictions that a human figure would appear particularly when human beings were in great need, and speak words of comfort to them.[15]

We have already seen how the title 'Son of Man' that Christ gave himself sums up the fact that he is our future — that what 'comes again,' the divine-human being of Jesus Christ, is both outside and within us, both strange and utterly familiar.

At the founding of The Christian Community, this insight played an important part. The founders wondered about the connection of this new movement to the Apostolic Succession, the teaching of the Roman Catholic Church that every bishop has been consecrated by the laying on of hands by a previous bishop, in an unbroken line back to Saint Peter, who was himself consecrated by Christ. This belief in the line of succession that links the church to the events of Christ's lifetime is one of the 'marks' of the true church according to Catholic teaching.

There was never any likelihood that a Catholic bishop might be part of the foundation of The Christian Community, but there was a feeling that a Catholic priest would at least have provided some contact with the stream of the succession. When Rudolf Steiner was asked, he told the founders that their task was to found a future succession. They were to connect, not to the historic events of two thousand years ago, but to the future reality of Christ's becoming accessible in a new way, which was and is already breaking into our present.

The path that leads into the communion service, the Act of Consecration of Man, is a path towards oneness with Christ as he appears today. In this way, all those who participate fully in the Act of Consecration are participants in the *parousia.*

This is what Paul means when he calls the cosmic Christ, the divine *Logos,* the head of the church. As we have seen, the word used for church in the New Testament is *ekklesia,* literally, the assembly called out. The church is called out of the world not to be apart from the world but to be a forerunner, a light on the hill, the yeast that makes the whole jar of meal rise. Just as the first Christians experienced a calling to witness to the living reality of Christ as they had seen and heard him, we are called to an experience of Christ that has the potential to transform the world. Just as the knowledge of the danger of idolatry is a negative test for the community, something to avoid, this image of community as first-fruits gives it its purpose.

Standing in Auschwitz confronted me with what the world can be — and Auschwitz of course is only one place, a point of concentration for the working of the most evil powers, which have been at work in countless other places before and since then. Every celebration of the new community is an icon of what the world can also be, a counterpart to Auschwitz.

8. The Way into the New Community

The journey of humanity and individual human beings into the new community is described in the longest and perhaps best-loved of Jesus' parables — the parable of the lost or prodigal son. This tells the story of a young man who goes on a journey of losing and finding himself. Once he has discovered that to become himself means being prepared to offer himself, he can enter into a new communion with his father at a sacrificial meal celebrating life born from death.

> Jesus said, 'There was a man who had two sons. The younger of them said to his father, "Father, give me the share of the property that will belong to me." So he divided his property between them. A few days later the younger son gathered all he had and travelled to a distant country, and there he squandered his property in dissolute living. When he had spent everything, a severe famine took place throughout that country, and he began to be in need. So he went and hired himself out to one of the citizens of that country, who sent him to his fields to feed the pigs. He would gladly have filled himself with the pods that the pigs were eating; and no one gave him anything. But when he came to himself he said, "How many of my father's hired servants have bread enough and to spare, but here I am dying of hunger! I will get up and go to my father, and I will say to him, 'Father, I have sinned against heaven and before you; I am no longer worthy to be called your son; treat me like one of your hired servants'." So he set off and went to his father. But while he was still far off, his father saw him and was filled with compassion; he ran and put his arms around

him and kissed him. Then the son said to him, "Father, I have sinned against heaven and before you; I am no longer worthy to be called your son." But the father said to his slaves, "Quickly, bring out a robe — the best one — and put it on him; put a ring on his finger and sandals on his feet. And get the sacrificial calf and kill it, and let us eat and celebrate; for this son of mine was dead and is alive again; he was lost and is found!" And they began to celebrate.

'Now his elder son was in the field; and when he came and approached the house, he heard music and dancing. He called one of the slaves and asked what was going on. He replied, "Your brother has come, and your father has killed the fatted calf, because he has got him back safe and sound." Then he became angry and refused to go in. His father came out and began to plead with him. But he answered his father, "Listen! For all these years I have been working like a slave for you, and I have never disobeyed your command; yet you have never given me even a young goat so that I might cele-brate with my friends. But when this son of yours came back, who has devoured your property with prostitutes, you killed the fatted calf for him!" Then the father said to him, "Son, you are always with me, and all that is mine is yours. But we had to celebrate and rejoice, because this brother of yours was dead and has come to life; he was lost and has been found".'

(Luke 15:11–32, NRSV modified)

The climax of the story is the moment when the father greets the son and welcomes him into a new communion with him. When we hear that he runs out to meet the son even before he has arrived home we gain a glimpse into the depth of his love. This love was ready to give everything away, not knowing whether the son would return. It recognizes in generosity what the son has become. This costly, risky love is at the heart of the whole of creation.

What has made the younger son ready to enter into this new community with the Father? The question presses on us all the more closely when we feel the justice of the older son's complaint. All earthly justice is indeed overturned by the father's action when he seems to prefer the wastrel to the dutiful child. A little background knowledge of the Ancient Near East makes this all the plainer. It was unheard of for a son to ask for his share before his father died: it would have meant mortgaging the estate, because the wealth would have been tied up in the land. This in turn meant that the value of the estate — for which a father had spent his life working — was effectively halved. It was as if the younger son had said: soon you'll be dead, and I don't care about the future of what you have worked for. Just give me my share! It would have been a scandal and a talking point in the whole neighbourhood.

Something happened through the journey of the younger son which was more important than all of this. The key is the moment in the pig field when he changes direction. When the famine arrives, the young man loses everything — all his money, and all the boon companions of the wild days which it bought. More serious than any outer loss, he loses a cherished image. Behind his wild living lay the conviction that this was a good life. The famine in the land must seem to the young man only a reflection of the famine within him — of the fact that his idea of the good life only led him to use everything up. Now his thoughts have become like the husks he feeds to the pigs — hard shells that need to be cracked open.

This moment marks a turning-point in our experience as readers. We know all too well the path that leads to the moment in the pig-field. It follows the law of this world — people will be selfish and they will squander what they get through their selfishness. Everything that comes after seems utterly surprising. We experience the transition from the law of this world to some other lawfulness. What happens in this moment gives the young man the power to *turn* more fully than he ever did before. Rudolf Bultmann once said that the defining characteristic of human beings was their 'radical openness' to the future. The young man has started to become more human, through becoming radically open to a new future.

The way into the self

The original Greek text reads literally: 'Then he went into himself.'

Where was he before?

Who is the he who went in, and who was the he that was living wildly?

What did he meet inside himself, that was himself?

The prodigal son becomes aware how his idea of the good life has led him to this desert. This devastating recognition strangely brings a kind of affirmation. Within him is one whom he had not yet known. This familiar stranger sees with him how he has strayed from his path and opens him for a new direction for his will.

Then he sees the future. He sees himself taking on a different role, voluntarily renouncing the status he had so scandalously abused, becoming a servant of his father, and no longer a mere recipient of gifts.

Of course we could interpret the parable at this point as meaning that the young man will return to become as dutiful as his older brother; but if this were so, the way the father welcomes him back into a new communion of table fellowship would make no sense. There are two aspects in his resolve to become a servant: on the one hand, in a society as concerned with status as was the Ancient Near East, it is a step of self-abasement, nearly as scandalous as the insult he inflicted on his father. On the other hand, his wish to be a servant means that he wants to be a co-worker, a sharer in the aims of his father who works to see that they will be fulfilled.

Both of these aspects resonate strongly with the being and the deed of the one telling the parable, whom Paul described in his Letter to the Philippians:

> Who, being in very nature God, did not consider equality
> with God something to be grasped, but made himself
> nothing, taking the very nature of a servant, being made
> in human likeness. And being found in appearance as a
> man, he humbled himself and became obedient to death
> — even death on a cross!
> (Philippians 2:6–9, NIV)

Again and again, when Jesus spoke of his Passion, he recalled the strange and beautiful prophecies about a servant of the Lord who will be despised, scourged and mocked. Again and again, even his closest disciples did not understand. They had not yet been opened as radically as the young man in the parable.

What the young man meets when he enters into himself in the depths of dereliction and despair is his true being. This true self is one with Christ, who is both within him and outside of him — 'myself, and yet someone other.' All the waste and suffering that the young man has been through have led him to the moment when his true humanity has been born. In fact it almost seems that he has guided himself into the situation that he needed to make this step. His longing to be a servant of his father is an intuition of his true destination and calling: to become Christ-like.

Paul, who knew well what force was needed to arrest someone on their self-determined path and get him to change course, speaks of this in his letter to the Colossians:

> You have died, and your life is hidden with Christ in
> God. When Christ who is your life is revealed, then you
> also will be revealed with him in glory.
> (Colossians 3:3–4, NRSV)

After the moment of crisis, when he entered himself, the young man achieves a kind of peace. At the beginning of the story when he snatches at his inheritance and then squanders it, it is hard to imagine him as peaceful, as he is so at odds with reality. In the pig-field he is deeply distressed. Now that he has come into himself, he has an inkling of the future he is drawing towards him. Although outwardly he is still starving and dishonoured, inwardly he has found his direction for the first time.

The journey home

How different is his journey back! The parable gives us no details, but we know that he is penniless in a famine-struck land. He must be nearly starving; his passage along the road will be with the beggars and outcasts, thrust aside by the rich and prestigious — in whose company he had probably made his way there. I wonder whether he repeats the words he is going to say to his father almost like a mantra: 'Father, I have sinned before heaven and before you!' He has found meaning in his journey; even if he feels sad about what he has wasted, he knows that it is only through this journey that he came to himself.

The father's reaction is as unexpected and miraculous as the son's turning. His son returns broken, filthy, and outcast, but connected to his future, to his true self. The father has been bearing him in his heart all the time; he knows with a true parent's love when the moment of turning has happened, and hastens towards him. The son's return, and the step he has taken, is far more important to the father than the dishonour and difficulty that he has brought on the family. Now the father looks with him to the new world that can come into being through his having 'come into himself.' The four gifts embody this: sandals, which no servant would have worn; the ring that confers authority and places him back in the circle of the family; the cloak which shows he shares with his father the mantle of power and authority in the family, and the feast of communion.

The older son can only experience the loving, creative mercy of the father as injustice. Love him as the father might, he cannot change this; the older son experiences a painful mirror of what was lacking in his own life, which seems to have been rule-bound and dutiful rather than full of risk and creative. Even knowing that he still has the status of the eldest son — 'Everything I have is yours' — is not enough to compensate for this. It is clear that Jesus directed this part of the parable against those who thought themselves 'good' — those who were sure that they were in with God, and who looked down on 'sinners.'

This long and beautiful story contains the essence of what Jesus Christ taught and lived. In his teaching, his dealings with human beings and his living and dying, he shows us that to be truly human does not mean to have achieved a state of goodness, but to be on a journey towards the true self, which is capable of creative and self-giving love. In another story, the parable of the talents, the sinner is the one who just holds on to what he has received, not risking anything. Jesus, whom we tend to think of as always mild and loving, uses angry words for those who think they have attained a status of goodness or holiness. Even the rich young man whom Jesus loved, who can say that he has kept all the commandments — the rules — since he was a child, has to get moving: 'Sell all you have and give to the poor.' This instruction to let go even of his hard-won treasure makes him grow sad 'because he was very rich' (see Matthew 19:16-21). In the Gospel of Saint John, where we learn that he is called Lazarus, we hear that the young man whom Jesus loved grew ill, even to the point of dying. Even he, who has lived a 'good' life, has to go through the same experience as the young man in the parable, before the hard shell of his lower self is soft enough for him to let everything go, even his life. Only then can he be called back to life by the one who is his higher being, standing outside the tomb. Only then is he prepared for the deepest communion, for he, the beloved disciple, is present at the first celebration of new life from death, the Last Supper on Maundy Thursday.

Every treasure, inner and outer, is a dangerous trap. Much better to pour out one's being in the gift of precious ointment, as does the woman in Matthew 26:6–8, than to stand stiffly aside, judging out of abstract principles what the Master should do, with whom he should consort and how.

This parable applies equally to every human life and to the journey of the whole of creation. Our journey is away from the original unity, the simple gift. We cannot stay in it, even if we want to. The divine world assents in our going, for there is no other way to the new union, the community, than through freedom which is also a kind of enslavement to self, to lower powers. Everything is placed into our hands — everything depends on our being prepared to go into ourselves — to become open — to understand the mystery of the true self that lives in giving itself away.

In the Act of Consecration of Man, we celebrate the beginning of the new community with the divine world. The very starkness and simplicity of this service are understandable in light of this. It does not comfort human souls in the first instance, or fulfil social needs. It is a place where human beings today — who recognize how far we have come on our journey 'down,' and who see all around them the consequences of our giddy progress, our waste of the substance we were given — can experience the welcome that is there, the celebration of life born from death, the dignity of their task of service, freely chosen in self-giving love.

Life as a journey

The idea of the good human life as a journey of losing and finding was hard for the early church to grasp, as it is for us today. The earliest Christians experienced the newness of life brought about through baptism so deeply that it took some centuries for the church to come to terms with the idea that one might sin after baptism and still be a Christian. At first those who had sinned were simply excommunicated — shut out of the table fellowship. Gradually it became clear that there was no future for a church that consisted only of sinless people. The crises of the persecutions by the Romans brought things to a head. Although there were many heroic martyrs to faith, there were many too who compromised, obtaining a pardon by making a token offering to Caesar, or even buying a forged certificate saying that they had made the offering. Even amongst the clergy there were many who compromised by going into hiding or even making the offering. What was to happen to such people after the persecution had ended? Were they to be excluded forever from the church? And what was to be done about the prevalent practice of postponing baptism until one was on one's deathbed, out of recognition of the fact that it was impossible to avoid sinning?

Although the practice of confession, which grew up from the fourth century on, seems to give more room for movement, it still reflects a static view of sin; there is just the possibility of moving from one 'state' to another and back again, as the following words from the Council of Trent show:

> the justification of a sinner is … a translation from that
> state in which man is born a child of the first Adam to
> the state of grace and of the 'adoption of the sons'

(Romans 8:15) of God through the second Adam, Jesus Christ, our Saviour ... (Decree on Justification, Chapter 4: *DS*, 796)[16]

There was another idea of sin in the early church, which in the western tradition got lost in the dominant, static image of the 'state of grace.' We saw above how Irenaeus saw the words in Genesis 1:26 — 'Let us make man in our image; according to our likeness let us make him' — as the key to the nature of the human being. The 'image' is our fundamental nature, which bears the imprint of our origin as creatures of God. The 'likeness' is the aim towards which we are striving. On earth the image is obscured. This gives us the challenge and the chance of achieving the likeness through our moral struggles. The earth is a 'vale of soul-making,' as John Keats said.

We know these two views from our experience. Seized with a new idea, a new resolve, we often become quite static in our thinking. We think that our first flush of enthusiasm means we have achieved our aim. The first time we 'fall from grace' — whether it be by eating a cream cake, growing impatient with our child, or not managing the meditation we have taken on — we plunge into despair about whether we will be able to manage anything at all. Deep down we were expecting that our resolve would change our state; that we would suddenly be transformed. This lies at the root of hypocrisy: instead of embracing the fact that change is a process, we divide within ourselves and have to pretend that we have achieved the redeemed state. Then we start to look down on the sinners who are not yet so enlightened. A new resolve cannot suddenly change our state, but it can be the beginning of a journey. The very failings are part of the process; through them we grow stronger. By owning them, we can integrate them into our understanding of our self, and develop greater compassion for the failings of those around us.

Even Saint Augustine, one of the great defenders of the western theology of the states of sin and grace, echoes such thoughts, when he says in a famous passage: 'You have made us *toward* yourself, and our hearts are restless until they find their rest in you.' (1983, I 1, p. 15).

The Sacramental Consultation

The sacraments intensify what is already in the world as a potential through Christ's deed. This intensification gives us strength to grow towards that potential. As an icon, a living embodiment of the power towards which it points, the sacrament also inspires us to open ourselves to this power. In the Sacramental Consultation we can prepare in unique intensity the human vocation of service out of our true self.

The words of the Sacramental Consultation begin with a twofold command to 'learn.' This is the deepest affirmation of our possibility to continue, to progress on our path. They echo the word Christ speaks to the woman caught in adultery in John 8, who has been condemned to death by stoning. The image of the stones which her accusers want to use echoes the experience of the crushing weight of shame that we can feel when our thinking gets too static and we condemn ourselves. Jesus undermines the self-righteous certainty of the accusers by appealing to their conscience, and to the fact that each of them — like every other human being — has sinned on his path. Then he looks at the woman and says to her: 'I do not condemn you. Go, and sin no more!' What must she have felt in that moment? She had been brought there by men who were convinced that she should not be allowed to continue her journey; she was to be crushed into the earth. Now Jesus speaks to her, knowing full well what she has done, and shows her that he believes that she *can* 'go' — that she can continue on her path. Does she even realize that the very impossibility of the words 'sin no more' do not mean that from now on she should be superhuman, but rather that whatever strayings she may fall into, she will find the power ever and again to 'go'?

What the Sacramental Consultation instructs us to learn is the offering of thoughts. The form of the word 'thought' — the past participle of the verb 'to think' — reveals that thoughts have to do with the past. Thoughts are the finished product of thinking. In the imagery of the parable, they are husks. Again and again we have to acknowledge that our thoughts, our explanations of things, may have been right when we thought them, but that we need to let go of them so that we can think afresh about a person, a situation, or even our values in life. Knowing our mind — having our picture of reality sorted out — gives us a kind of security, but it proves ever and again to be inflexible or illusory.

The conversation or conversations with a priest that precede receiving the sacrament can be a help in clearing away thoughts so that living thinking can begin. Their form is not laid down; it is left to each individual to decide what he or she will bring into the conversation. The priest's primary role, particularly in the conversation which ends with the reading of the verse of the sacrament, is to listen. Any questions he or she asks may serve to loosen more layers of encrusted thought; they may be catalysts for finding the new thinking that can come when old thoughts are released. It should be stressed that the process takes place at the pace the person seeking the sacrament chooses. It can be quite shocking to think of letting go of all my familiar mental furniture in one go. This is not what is intended in the Consultation. Rather, by practising in the areas that seem most pressing, or indeed in those that feel the freest, such as giving thanks, we bring processes into movement into our soul that have an effect on the whole. We may find that we start to remember the words of the Consultation in everyday life, that they accompany us as we make decisions and have conversations with our fellow human beings.

It could that the longing to have children, or a partner, has taken on a fixed form, an image of myself surrounded by a loving family, which makes me devalue any other option in life. Here it might be important to become free of the thought that only such a life would bring fulfilment; to allow the longing for community of life and abundance to remain in my soul, but to become open about what form it will take. Or perhaps we have resigned ourselves to disappointment, concluding that reality is not as vivid and exciting as we hoped when we were young. 'My colleagues and I just can't understand each other' — this can become a fixed conclusion that shuts down any possibility for change. Have we resigned ourselves too fast? Are we shutting out the possibility of new life and transformation by our conviction, which offers a perverse kind of safety? — After all,

if it is true, then I don't have to expose myself to the risk of making renewed efforts. Or we may be plagued by the sense of guilt
about something that we did in the past. Again, the conclusion
that we have drawn, that it is all our fault, and that we hardly
deserve to carry on living, has a compelling power. Here it may
be important to look at the situation afresh, to understand my
part in it, and that of others. Out of this, new horizons may open
up; liberated from the crushing weight of guilt, I am freer to be
creative. Perhaps I can still make amends for what I've done; at
the very least, I can think the situation right for myself, and
learn from it how I would want to behave in a similar situation
in the future. The very experience of finding a standpoint from
which I can see what I have thought in a new light is a liberation
from the weight of the past.

When someone comes for the Sacramental Consultation,
there may be a particular life situation that stands in the fore-
ground. It is also good if the reason for coming is not a particular problem or question, but simply the wish to deepen our
participation in the Act of Consecration of Man. Some people
come regularly, perhaps before their birthday or in
Passiontide, in order to review their life and bring it consciously into the Act of Consecration of Man once again. In this
it becomes clear that the Sacramental Consultation is not the
same as psychotherapy. It is not primarily about curing problems — in fact if the 'thoughts' we have been speaking about
are too ingrained, and the one seeking the sacrament cannot
find inner freedom, then the priest may well suggest seeking
help from a counsellor or therapist. It is concerned rather with
leading over what we have experienced into the life of the
community in the Act of Consecration of Man — although of
course the content of the conversation is safeguarded with
complete confidentiality.

The next thing we are told to learn is to receive our will from
above. Once the hard shell of past thoughts has cracked open,
we can receive the will that comes from our true, highest being.
Sometimes this starts during the conversation, or when the
words of the sacrament are spoken. It is also possible to try to
hold on to the emptiness, the openness of mind and will, with
the feeling that the process of offering and receiving in the Act

of Consecration of Man, which should be attended as soon as possible following the Consultation, will complete it.

In the offering of thought and the receiving of will we can see a kind of metamorphosis of confession and penance. In the old confession, the penitents had to compare their behaviour with a list of sins, and see where they had gone wrong. Using an external authority, they found a yardstick for correcting their mistaken idea of what it was good to do. In the penance, an external authority — the priest — demanded from them that they school their will by submitting it to the will of the church in performing a symbolic punishment — reciting Hail Mary's, or praying the rosary a certain number of times. In speaking the formula 'I absolve you,' the priest released the penitent from the burden of the past. The church took on the burden; we might say that the church performed the offering of thoughts, and in doing this, renewed its connection to Christ.

By instructing the one seeking the sacrament to offer and receive, the Sacramental Consultation makes clear that the power of allowing sin to be transformed through offering and communion has now passed into the responsibility of every human being. For this reason there is no list of sins against which to compare our conduct. In our time it is more appropriate for human beings to examine their behaviour in the light of a living understanding of what they really are and what they truly want. This doesn't mean we have to work it out for ourselves — we may seek reflection from friends, colleagues and others. The conversation that precedes the Consultation can have this character too — the priest will try to listen in such a way that I can find my *real* questions. But it is *my* questions I have to find; I must ultimately answer for them, for it is *I* who will be told 'learn to offer.'

Forgiveness

The fact that the Consultation does not contain the old formula of absolution does not mean that it is not concerned with the forgiveness of sin. When Christ, who speaks through the sacraments, places his confidence in us to 'learn to offer' this can be a reminder that he has taken upon himself the load of human sinfulness, which would otherwise crush us. Forgiveness of sins does not mean that we are translated into a sinless state, with the slate wiped clean. This would deny the value of our journey. Nevertheless, our sins have consequences that we cannot change on our journey. In the parable, the father's estate has been mortgaged, and the capital used up; the young man's awakening to self-knowledge does not change that. My process of acknowledging where I have gone wrong, and even trying to compensate for it, cannot bring back what was hindered or harmed through my neglect or wilful destruction.

It is this objective, crushing weight that John the Baptist means when he says: 'Behold the lamb of God, who takes away the sins of the world' (John 1:29). Because Christ liberates us and the earth from the burden of sin he has the creative power to say: 'Your sins are forgiven ... Go!'

The old confession emphasized the release from the weight of past sin; the Sacramental Consultation emphasizes the new direction in life that is made possible by that release.

Through preparation and conversation, through the offering of thoughts and opening for the will that comes as a gift, we can enter into ourselves like the young man in the parable.

Where were we before?

Who is the 'we' that went in, and who was the 'we' that was living until that moment?

What do we meet inside ourselves, that is our true self?

The sacrament gives an answer to these questions in the sentences that follow. Letting go of thoughts and letting the future come towards us brings true peace into the soul. A new attitude towards the world can start to pervade us: we will see the world, and everything that we meet, as a revelation of the Spirit, as a part of God's glory. This will fill us with love for all those around us. Love will enter us as a force: love for God and love for humanity. In this most private and personal sacrament, the seed of new community is sown.

With these promises of what will occur, the Sacramental Consultation prophesies a new human being, one who lives so selflessly that he or she holds on to nothing; who is open for the divine will; whose soul-life is in perfect harmony; who sees the world as the revelation of the divine and whose whole being is irradiated with love. Do we know this human being? Pontius Pilate said, looking at the Suffering Servant being mocked, scourged and crowned in the purple through the jest of common soldiers: 'Behold the man! See what is truly human!' His words echo down the centuries. We do know this human being — it is Jesus Christ, the Son of Man, the representative of the future of humanity. The Sacramental Consultation is an apocalyptic sacrament, in the deepest sense. Apocalypse means the breaking open of the husk. Through the offering of thoughts, the husk that cuts us off from reality — from our true self — cracks open. We experience identity with our true selves, just as can happen in great moments of crisis in our lives, as happens to the younger son in the parable. We experience our deepest being, who is one with the Suffering Servant, with Christ.

As we saw earlier, in his poem, 'That Nature is a Heraclitean Fire,' Gerard Manley Hopkins describes a moment of crisis when everything that had seemed to give him security fell away from him, and all his assumptions about life were overturned. Then he says,

> In a flash, at a trumpet crash,
> I am all at once what Christ is, since he was what I am,
> and this Jack, joke, poor potsherd, patch, matchwood,
>   immortal diamond,
> *Is* immortal diamond.
> (1970, p. 106)

Every crisis, and every moment of turning such as we can experience through Sacramental Consultation, makes it possible for the immortal diamond of our true being to shine out in our lives.

The healing deed of Christ is so vast that there is no single image that can encompass it. We have to distinguish between different aspects that make up the whole. We saw above the importance of distinguishing the subjective and objective aspects of Christ's deed. On the one hand this deed brought about a change for all human beings, regardless of whether they know it, or know him. This utter objectivity is expressed in his bearing 'the sins of the world.' But it matters too that we know him. He is a symbol of the full potential of our humanity. Every exceptional human being makes something possible for human beings that was not possible before — on a trivial level, when Roger Bannister ran the first four-minute mile, suddenly all the top athletes could do it. But with Jesus this goes deeper. Because what he lives is the essence of true humanity, his example does more than just show us what is possible; it unlocks the power of our humanity within us.

The Sacramental Consultation places before us the image of our true self. This image beckons us to fulfil our potential. It is not merely an image outside of us, though: it unfolds the power within us to be that which we truly are. This true human being is the one who can take part in the great service of the offering of thoughts, the opening to the future, in the celebration of life born from death. Through coming into himself the young man in the parable is able to join in table-fellowship with his father at the sacrificial meal, celebrating new life born from death; our coming into ourselves makes us able to become ever more fully part of the meal that celebrates the new life given to us by Christ.

Ever and again we are tempted to think that we need to perfect ourselves before we can join the meal — like the early Christians, postponing baptism to their deathbeds, in case they might sin. It is far more challenging to realize that I am welcome as I am — as Jack, joke, poor potsherd — as long as I remain open to the voice that says 'Go — sin no more — learn!'

When the Son of Man erupted on to the scene of the ancient world, all the old assumptions were overturned. All the hardened thoughts about what it means to be 'good,' to be 'holy,' were exposed as husks. Those who were able to find living thinking could receive him into their hearts. In our time Christ is becoming present in a new way, as countless human beings have witnessed. His coming today is different from his coming two thousand years ago. It has in common with the first coming, though, that it needs the complete overturning of our familiar mental frameworks. '*Metanoite!*' says John the Baptist. 'Change your mind — expand your consciousness — become cosmic again!' Today his call sounds again — a word of flame that ignites a fire in our soul that brings everything into movement. Nicholas Peter Harvey writes:

> The power and the threat of Jesus lie in his capacity to call the true self of each of us out of repression and hiding. The whole thrust of his life is to awaken us, his brothers and sisters, to the place in ourselves which is open to the living God, with all the surprise and unlearning that awakening entails. (Harvey 1991, p. 104)

The apocalypse of the true self that yearns for its fulfilment in service is the centre of the Sacramental Consultation. It prepares us and invites us to join in the communion meal where we experience the embrace of Christ, who celebrates new life with us who are lost and are found again and again, who are dead and experience the power of rebirth through this encounter again and again.

We do not need mystical experiences to know this — the Sacramental Consultation is that encounter. It is both a promise of what we can become, and a reminder of how far we have to go.

The divine pedagogy

In experiencing the Sacramental Consultation, we can experience that to be human means to be in a process of becoming. Origen saw the world as the place where human beings are educated. We are here to learn and progress, so that we may conform in the end to the image in which we were created. It was clear to him that this journey would take many cycles of time, and would involve many lifetimes. This idea was one of the teachings for which he was condemned after his death. The idea of reincarnation was blotted out of Christian thinking. This can seem as big a mystery as the rejection of the idea of the human spirit, to which it is related. A world-historic necessity is at work in this rejection. The old knowledge of reincarnation led human beings to devalue the immediacy of this earthly life. The uniqueness and the responsibility of every human life had to be learnt.

Even today when people hear about reincarnation, it can be tempting to use it as an excuse — 'we can sort that out next time.' This shows how important it is to think about reincarnation in a moral way. If we are able to do this, there need be no conflict with Christianity.[17] Perhaps it is less important to try to decide on the truth of this idea than to test its usefulness in life. If I feel on the one hand that I can progress and that this progress is meaningful, and am aware on the other hand that I am unlikely fully to achieve my aim in one lifetime, it is a comfort and a source of strength to imagine that there are other lifetimes in which I will be able to continue my work.

9. The Act of Consecration of Man — the Celebration of the New Community

'Do you see our Sun, do you see Him?'
    'I am afraid ... I dare not look,' whispered Alyosha.
    'Do not fear Him. He is terrible in His greatness, awful in His sublimity, but infinitely merciful. He has made Himself like unto us from love and rejoices with us. He is changing the water into wine that the gladness of the guests may not be cut short. He is expecting new guests. He is calling new ones unceasingly forever and ever. ... There they are bringing new wine. Do you see, they are bringing the vessels ...'
    (Dostoevsky 2002, p. 941)

The meal

Again and again, the gospels show Jesus sharing meals with people who were the outcasts of society — tax-collectors, 'sinners' and prostitutes. This was a great scandal for the official representatives of religion — those who thought themselves 'good.' The ancient world was concerned about ritual pollution in much the same way as we are about germs today. There was little idea of infectious illness, but ritual impurity was seen as infectious. If one had become unclean by touching something or someone polluted, one was excluded from the ritual community. This is the background to the behaviour of the priest and the Levite who crossed the road to avoid the man left for dead in the parable of the Good Samaritan (Luke 10:25–37). They did not want to incur the ritual pollution of touching a dead body.

Jesus was not just careless about such matters; he seems to have preferred the society of the ritually impure, if they were open for community with him. He not only associated with them, he loved to sit at table with them — sharing on the most intimate level. Their awareness of their own brokenness made them open for community with the one who could make them whole. When the prodigal son became a swineherd, he made himself as impure as possible. Spending time with pigs — even longing to eat their food — he was outside the ritual community. Only in this destitution could he come 'into himself.' Jesus' table-guests had reached similar moments of coming 'into themselves' through their path in life and were ready to be part of a new communion.

The meal is the most basic building-block of community. Hunger is the fundamental, inescapable factor of human life, the basis of all economics, and of all community. In lifting the brute need for food, without which we could not live, into the realm of shared life, we dignify it. We are all dependent on food; by sharing we make ourselves vulnerable and allow others to witness our need; by sharing we bring humanity and grace into this realm of life where the harshest necessity holds sway.

From ancient times, worshippers shared meals with their gods. Human beings, who had received their being from the gods, were required to offer something back, not just to keep for themselves what sustained them. Otherwise the gift given by the gods would have been lost to the gods for ever. Only through thanksgiving freely offered could the gift be returned in an act of communion. When the offering was burned as a sacrifice, the god was 'nourished' by receiving the etherealized essence, the 'pleasing fragrance' that was released. The circulation of glory was completed. It is strange and somehow unsettling to think that the spiritual world needs the offering we bring. In the overflowing generosity of his self-bestowal in creation, God has made himself dependent on us. We have taken his substance, and everything depends on our not wasting the gift in 'riotous living,' but turning freely towards the service of the higher world.

When Jesus shared his meals with outcasts and 'sinners' it was both a concrete, historical deed and a symbol. These meals were an anticipation of the royal banquet in the Kingdom of God. He wanted his table-fellowship to be seen as a living embodiment, an icon of the Kingdom. All are invited, 'both bad and good,' as it says in the parable of the kingly wedding in Matthew 22. The decision whether to be a part of this communion, in company one had not perhaps expected, rested with the individual. Those who were too busy being scandalized by the overthrow of the rules, who counted themselves already part of the Kingdom, excluded themselves from communion, like the elder son in the parable of the prodigal son.

Letting go and letting come

The Sacramental Consultation reveals the future human being as one who has come into himself and who longs to serve. In the Act of Consecration of Man, human beings can join in a service of the divine world. What follows is not intended to be an exhaustive description of the Act of Consecration, which is given elsewhere in the literature of The Christian Community, but a pathway through it from the particular viewpoint of this book.[18]

In the Offering, the second part of the Act of Consecration, we may let go of all that is in our soul. In order to do this, we acknowledge that what separates us from our true being flows to the divine ground. This confession is spoken by the priest in the 'I'-form. Everyone present is free to identify with it as far as they wish. It can be a good moment to remember whatever crusts have been loosened and allowed to 'flow' through our preparation for participating in the Act of Consecration, perhaps in a Sacramental Consultation. Every encrusted thought and attitude, every compelling habit, every hurt and grievance; even living with the wish to release all this, and to be released from it, helps the 'flow.' Then we can consciously turn the positive forces of our soul to the divine world, and watch as they are embodied by water and wine being poured into the cup.

All of this echoes what has been the practice of offering since before the beginning of history. It is described most fully in the Old Testament, for example in the Book of Leviticus:

> The LORD called Moses, and spoke to him from the tent
> of meeting, saying, 'Speak to the people of Israel, and say
> to them, When any man of you brings an offering to the
> LORD, you shall bring your offering of cattle from the
> herd or from the flock. If his offering is a burnt offering
> from the herd, he shall offer a male without blemish; he
> shall offer it at the door of the tent of meeting, that he
> may be accepted before the LORD; he shall lay his hand
> upon the head of the burnt offering, and it shall be
> accepted for him to make atonement for him. Then he
> shall kill the bull before the LORD; and Aaron's sons the
> priests shall present the blood, and throw the blood
> round about against the altar that is at the door of the
> tent of meeting. And he shall flay the burnt offering and
> cut it into pieces; and the sons of Aaron the priest shall
> put fire on the altar, and lay wood in order upon the fire;
> and Aaron's sons the priests shall lay the pieces, the
> head, and the fat, in order upon the wood that is on the
> fire upon the altar; but its entrails and its legs he shall
> wash with water. And the priest shall burn the whole on
> the altar, as a burnt offering, an offering by fire, a pleas-
> ing odour to the LORD.' (Leviticus 1:1–9)

When we read such a passage, we realize that for the ancient
Jewish people, the identification between the inner and the
outer worlds was far stronger than it is for us. The Old
Testament traces the process by which outer values become interior ones. By the time of the prophets, it was clear that any outer
offering needs to have its counterpart in an inner offering.
Today, our offering is of a purely inner nature. With this in mind,
we can find the correspondence between the descriptions of
offering in the Old Testament and our own offering. The bull
offered in the passage quoted would correspond to our willing;
offerings of a lamb to our feeling, and the offering of a dove to
an element of our thinking. The descriptions of offering in the
Old Testament can be a kind of handbook for us, if we can
'translate' the outer things used into inner soul-qualities. They
describe in unparalleled fullness the practice — we might even
say the technology — of offering.

We can try to imagine the situation of the tribal elder who makes the offering of the best bull of the herd — an object of immense value, in whose loins the whole future of the herd was contained. What a temptation it must have been to choose a bull with even a small blemish! Every rational instinct of a stock-breeder would tell him not to kill the beast that represented the future prosperity of the tribe. The benefit experienced must have been great indeed, to justify what in earthly terms seemed a scandalous waste.

What must it have felt like to watch as the form of the animal offered dissolved in the flames, and its earthly potential was consumed? All that is left is the space where the beast had been standing. In this space there is a particular kind of emptiness. For a view of the world that saw in everything earthly the condensation of spiritual processes, to give something over to the fire in the right way was to release spiritual forces that had been trapped in their earthly embodiment.

The tribal elder who brought the offering knew that the apparently empty space where the bull had been standing was not empty at all — it was a place of potential, where a stream of blessing could flow. This blessing alone could ensure the future of the tribe.

The first half of the Offertory in the Act of Consecration follows the ancient pattern. There is the 'sin offering,' which we have already spoken of — the acknowledgment of what has already flowed to God. Then there is the threefold offering, of will, feeling and thought. The wine is poured as an embodiment of the willing that is offered to the Father; the water embodies the feeling that is united with Christ. If we were following the service with analytical eyes, we might ask: where then is the third substance, the substance for the Holy Spirit? In fact the Spirit is at work in the mixing and mingling of water and wine. This very mixing is the embodiment of our thinking, which combines divine and earthly realities.

The mixture of water and wine is raised up as a drink for God, as a 'pleasing fragrance to the Lord.' The earthly world is lifted up to become nourishment which makes a new communion with the divine world possible. *Koinonia,* the gift of the Holy Spirit, has made us partners, stakeholders, sharers in a common substance that has been offered. Everyone present has a share in what is mixed in the cup. Now that it is offered to the divine world, we can feel that our community of life has been opened to the *koinonia* of the Trinity. The bond of love of the Holy Spirit, which unites lover and beloved and allows them to live in each other, has begun to extend from the earthly to spiritual world.

Now there is a turning point. In the first half of the Offertory, until the raising of the cup and its pleasing fragrance, we can feel ourselves in the company of human beings since the beginning of history — those who brought offerings even though they did not yet know Christ. However, the offering of the Act of Consecration is not an Old Testament offering. Six centuries before Christ, the old system of offering already needed to be revised. In the Book of Jeremiah, Yahweh speaks: 'What do I care about incense from Sheba or sweet calamus from a distant land? Your burnt offerings are not acceptable; your sacrifices do not please me.' (Jeremiah 6:20, NIV).

By the sixth century BC, human beings were already so separate from what was performed before them that there was a risk of their simply following empty forms. The Psalmist wrote: 'The sacrifices of God are a broken spirit; a broken and contrite heart, O God, you will not despise' (Psalm 51:17, NIV). What is the sacrifice of a broken heart and a contrite spirit, other than what happens on the pig field, the moment of opening when we can go 'into ourselves'? The old way of offering depended on human beings not being quite in themselves — feeling that their individual existence dissolved in the offering flame. To follow this path today would contradict our need to tread the path towards selfhood.

This is the central paradox of human evolution. Our journey takes us away from the original unity. But if this journey were continued to its conclusion, where we would be completely cut off from the spirit, there would be no hope for human beings — for our true being is spiritual, and without a new connection to the spirit, we cannot become what we are destined to be.

This is the mystery of Christ's self-offering. The sacrificial system of the ancient world came to an end because it rested on a path that could not be united with the tendency towards selfhood. Human beings could no longer submerge themselves in a unity that recalled the original unity. The ancient principle of sacrifice overcame the tendency towards separation. We can imagine the tribe watching as the chief offered the bull. The very sight of the beast's violent death, the smell of its blood, must have jolted those who witnessed it out of themselves. The principle of Christian sacrifice could not be more different. The path to joining in the sacrifice of the one who is my true self lies through finding my true self. After the middle of the Offertory, it becomes clear that this path of offering is radically different from what went before. After this turning-point, we pray that Christ may take our offering into his own self-offering. The new way of losing myself means that I find my true self — the one which is hidden with Christ in the spiritual world, the one who offers himself in us and with us.[19]

The Letter to the Hebrews makes it clear that the ancient offerings were reflections of the archetype of the sacrifice of Christ that underlies reality. Christ's sacrifice on Golgotha is once and for all, because it is no mere reminder of the sacrifice at the centre of things, but the translation of that sacrifice on to the stage of history. If the sacrificial services before Christ were reflections of his deed, and preparation for his coming, the services of offering and sacrifice since Golgotha serve to make it real and present.

One of the great questions that raged in the Reformation was whether the Mass is a repetition of the sacrifice that Christ made on Golgotha, or a memorial of it. To see in it a repetition takes away from the uniqueness, the once for all quality of Christ's deed. But if the Mass is only a memorial, is there any real reason to perform it as an earthly, sacramental reality? Would it not be as good — or better even — just to meditate on Christ's deed? This is the mystery of sacramental working. It is neither memorial nor repetition; rather it makes ever more real — more *actual* — what has been inaugurated as *potential*. In this moment when we have opened ourselves through our offering, and so freed ourselves from time, the timeless reality of Christ's sacrifice can become more present, more real in time again. We join in the great work of transforming the world because he is at work in us. And this is possible through the work of the Holy Spirit who connects what we do on earth with its counterpart in the world of spirit, the world of our origins.

The final words of the Offertory are a prayer that a fire of love may be ignited in our offering. Everything that we offered — the crusts that were released, the highest soul-forces that we consciously turned — is consumed. What can happen for individuals through the Sacramental Consultation happens here as a community process. Wherever each individual may be on his or her journey, the community as a whole goes through a process of losing and finding, of dying and becoming. All that we brought into the offering is consumed by the fire. Christ himself goes once more into the fire of death. A special kind of space is created where everything that has been offered is no longer. Just as the empty space where the bull had stood was a receptive space, open for blessing, we can feel that an opening has been created through the sacrificial fire.

The third part of the Act of Consecration begins with the counterpart to the blessing that the tribe received through the sacrifice of the prize beast. Our offering, which has become part of the eternal offering of Christ, has been consumed. Everything specific and particular in it has been dissolved. It passes back into the state of the beginning, when it was infolded in God, and existed only as pure potential. It is also a foretaste of the future state, where everything that has taken on particular form will lose it, in order to exist as the 'stuff' of resurrection, in its essence. Now it rays back to us as blessing. The whole of the third part of the Act of Consecration is drenched in this stream of blessing. If we have made real for ourselves that something of our own being was united with the offering made at the altar, and has been consumed in the fire, then the blessing stream can stream into the space that was created in our own soul.

This power of blessing that streams to us from the future makes possible the central mystery of the Act of Consecration, the transformation of bread and wine into body and blood. This is the ultimate expression of the new community between heaven and earth, between God and humanity. Before the final prayer that the bread and wine may become Christ's body and blood, we pray that the grace of the Holy Spirit may stream down in a great movement from heaven to earth, meeting the stream that flows in our offering from earth to heaven. If we meditate on this moment, we are drawn deeper into the mystery — for whose power is it that makes us able to bring the offering and to perceive the working of the spiritual in the earthly world? — it is the power of the Holy Spirit. Spirit meets spirit in the mutually interpenetrating and enhancing streams that flow between the altar and the heavens.

Finally, in the fourth part of the Act, the Communion, we are invited to take the transformed substances into ourselves. Just as any true meal — indeed any act of sharing — rests on mutual giving and receiving, the Communion is a mutual bestowal and accepting of each other. We tend of course to focus on the challenge of making it real for ourselves that we receive Christ in the Communion. Another challenge is to understand that he receives something from us — that Communion is an exchange. Perhaps it is easiest to understand this if we think of communion as a conversation. In a true conversation each conversation-partner is enriched by what the other brings. And in this we recognize the work of the Spirit of connection, of interpenetration, of mutual bestowal and receiving.

Seven times throughout the Act of Consecration of Man the priest turns around and says to the community 'Christ in you.' The one we behold before us at the altar is within us; we are within him. It can be hard to realize this — to feel the immortal diamond among all the potsherds of our every day existence. We cannot earn the gift of his presence in us, but we can prepare for him to enter us, and to come alive as the power of our true being within us. Thinking again of preparation for Communion and the kind of self-examination that we can undergo, we realize that no list of sins against which to compare our conduct could be as powerful as the question: what hinders me from conforming to the image of my true being that I see before me at the altar? What can I bring into movement, so that I can join in the great cycle of offering and receiving; so that I can be at peace, see the world as revelation, and be perfectly open for love which I radiate as freely as I receive it?

The sun amongst the seven sacraments

The Act of Consecration of Man occupies a central place in the organism of the seven sacraments in The Christian Community. It is the activity of the community itself. The other sacraments help individuals on their path in life at decisive moments. The Act of Consecration creates the substance which flows into them and makes their blessing power possible.

The Act of Consecration begins with the exhortation that all who are present may fulfil it worthily. It is a great moment in the development of the Christian liturgy, when the whole congregation is invited to be a part of the objective event that is to unfold at the altar. Each of the other sacraments is given in a moment when we stand before a threshold — the threshold of birth and death, and the threshold of puberty; the threshold of the great decisions to marry or to become a priest. These moments are unique in a human biography. The fact that we can decide to attend the Act of Consecration of Man every week, even every day in larger congregations, should not take away from the fact that it is a threshold which is just as great, even if it can be repeated. That is why the Sacramental Consultation — uniquely among the other sacraments — can be repeated to help us in our decision to cross the threshold into the Act of Consecration.

As an icon of the new community, the Act of Consecration of Man contains iconic symbols. The priest wears the chasuble, which has two very different symbols on front and reverse sides. For most of the service, the congregation looks at the reverse, with the symbol of a great 'U.' There is no single 'right' interpretation of this, no secret code encrypted there; but we might see in it a trace of the journey from our original unity with God 'down' into material existence and back again. Like every true symbol, this can be seen on many different levels. Every day, every human life, and the whole journey of human evolution are such journeys. The symbol on the front of the chasuble has quite a different character. It is a lemniscate, a kind of figure 8. In this symbol, a higher and a lower realm are joined. They remain distinct, and yet they flow into each other and interpenetrate each other.

These two symbols complement each other. At every point

on the 'U,' the lemniscate is also there as a possibility. Wherever we are on our journey — as individuals, or as humanity, we are not trapped in the lower realm, but we can always pray for the joining of the realms — for community. This is expressed too in the words of the Act of Consecration of Man that speak of the offerings brought to God by those 'who had not yet Christ.' In the Act of Consecration of Man we join with the whole of humanity as it has made offerings to unite the lower and the higher realms since the beginning of history.

There is another aspect of the Act of Consecration of Man that distinguishes it from the other sacraments. It is never revealed in its totality. It is a process that unfolds through time. Each festival season has its seasonal prayer, and each week has its gospel reading. In this way too it is like the sun of the solar system of the seven sacraments: from day to day, week to week and month to month we experience a different aspect of the sun's rays, and a different quality of light.[20] Every week, the Act of Consecration brings a new aspect of the present-day working of Christ to us.

10. The Biographical Path in the Community of Christ

The earliest Christians saw becoming a member of the community not as a change of status but as the beginning of a new life — the life of the new Adam going on parallel to the life of the natural Adam. Saint Paul describes it using images drawn both from the Old Testament and from the initiations of the ancient mysteries.

> As therefore you received Christ Jesus the Lord, so live in him, rooted and built up in him and established in the faith, just as you were taught, abounding in thanksgiving. ... For in him the whole fullness of deity dwells bodily, and you have come to fullness of life in him, who is the head of all rule and authority. In him also you were circumcised with a circumcision made without hands, by putting off the body of flesh in the circumcision of Christ; and you were buried with him in baptism, in which you were also raised with him through faith in the working of God, who raised him from the dead. And you, who were dead in trespasses and the uncircumcision of your flesh, God made alive together with him, having forgiven us all our trespasses, having cancelled the bond which stood against us with its legal demands.
> (Colossians 2:6–12)

The circumcision was the rite of entry into the people of God in the Old Testament. In the very place on which the future of the race depended, the male reproductive organ, an opening is made through a wound being inflicted. The deeper, sacramental meaning can be seen in the fact that when a child is born without a foreskin, or the foreskin has had to be removed as part of surgical procedure, the ritual circumcision is achieved with a pinprick in the head of the organ. If the bloodstream has been opened, circumcision has taken place.

The prophets experienced a deeper, inner meaning of circumcision. The heart is covered over with a carapace and is no longer open to the words of the living God. The heart needs to be circumcised before it can be the organ of faith in Yahweh.

Now, in the letter to the Colossians, the entire bodily existence has become the carapace. The rite of baptism means setting aside the natural man, the 'first man,' and laying open the entire inner existence, the second man, for the influence of Christ.

If the image of circumcision is powerful, what follows is even more so. 'Buried with him in baptism' — what can Saint Paul mean by this? How did the experience of baptism become transparent for an experience of death? In some remarkable paintings of Christ's baptism in the Jordan from the earliest days of the church, a meaning which has since been quite forgotten shines through. Christ's descent into the river is shown as a battle with the demon of the deep. In the Old Testament, the depths are the place of chaos, of the adversary forces. In creation, God brings order into the threatening powers of chaos. The Psalmist and Jonah describe the journey to the depths, where the experience of being overwhelmed by water becomes transparent for an inner experience of initiation.

> I called to the Lord, out of my distress, and he answered me; out of the belly of the pit I cried, and thou didst hear my voice. For thou didst cast me into the deep, into the heart of the seas, and the flood was round about me; all thy waves and thy billows passed over me. Then I said, 'I am cast out from thy presence; how shall I again look upon thy holy temple?' The waters closed in over me, the deep was round about me; weeds were wrapped about my head at the roots of the mountains. I went down to the land whose bars closed upon me for ever; yet thou didst bring up my life from the Pit, O Lord my God. (Jonah 2:2–6, RSV altered)

Christian neophytes had a similar experience when they approached baptism. They buried their earthly being with Christ and were raised with him. Just like neophytes in the mysteries, the Christians realized that they were dead in their former existence; that they had come to new life through their encounter with Christ. What is new was that their encounter with the living God was at the same time the encounter with one who had lived historically.

Baptism

In The Christian Community, the process of entering the community takes place in three moments separated by a number of years. The first moment is an infant baptism. It seems to have little in common with the dramatic, life changing ritual of Baptism in the early church described above. Through the infant baptism, the child is taken into the womb of the church. The godparents — in German, *Wächter,* which means 'guardians' or 'watchers' — and indeed the whole congregation, take on to watch over the child's development and to pray for it. A part of this task is religious instruction.

In the ancient church, members were only admitted into the church after they had made their own conscious decision to become a part of it, and gone through adult baptism. Quickly, however, children started to be baptized. As they could not answer for themselves, godparents swore the oaths in their name. What had been undertaken on their behalf was confirmed when they came of age — in the ancient world, at around the time of puberty.

The infant Baptism practised in The Christian Community is addressed to the needs of the child. The prenatal time is a recapitulation of paradise, where the embryo is sheltered and nourished from outside. The soul of the newborn child experiences through the sudden meeting with gravity, cold and hunger an echo of our excommunication from the oneness of our origin. Baptism is a counterpart: a welcome into a community that is striving towards the new unity.

A particular part is played by three substances: water, salt and ash. Here, the idea that everything we meet in the world is a cooled-down spark of the original glory becomes real. The words spoken over the three substances reconnect them to the processes from which they have condensed — the same processes the alchemists studied in deep meditation as *sal, mercur* and *phosphor*. Through the working of the Holy Spirit, earthly substance is reconnected to the spiritual process of its origin. The child meets a reminder of our origin in the unity with the spirit, and a foretaste of the world to come.

Confirmation

The Sacrament of Confirmation contains the second part of the baptism in the early church, the bestowal of the Holy Spirit. Confirmation is the biographical gateway into the Act of Consecration. The Sacrament of Confirmation contains many elements of the original unified baptism of early Christianity. There is an intense period of preparation. The confirmands are told that they are on the threshold from one period of life to the next. They are confronted with their mortality — the service refers to the 'moment of death.' They are endowed with the Holy Spirit in a laying on of hands. But is there something that corresponds to the moment of initiation — the encounter with the chaotic powers of the deep, the threefold questioning and confession and the passage from darkness to light? Just as the 'gestation' of the infant in the womb of the church now follows infant Baptism, this 'initiation' follows Confirmation. In the Confirmation, a process is begun which is completed in life by the confirmands themselves. They are introduced to Christ as the light they must now seek themselves. After the blessing they are released into life — at first the life of the Act of Consecration of Man, but then into the life of the world. Jonah's cry from the depths reminds us of the experience of being an adolescent — a victim of the surging powers of life that the teenager feels. Jonah's story embodies the heights and depths of the soul world through which the teenager passes.

The renewed sacraments do not come at the end of a

process, but rather inaugurate something whose fulfilment lies in the future. The single dramatic moment has become a biographical process. So does Saint Paul's imagery no longer apply? Putting aside the old man, releasing the heart from its hardened carapace — these are things which at first do not seem to be relevant to the teenager. It is easy to think that it is too soon to speak of such things. However, the years between Confirmation and full adulthood are crucial. A young woman once put a question which showed how crucial: she asked, why is it that my friends have lost their longing for a better world, for a true and nobler life? Why have they settled for so little? Adolescence marks the beginning of liberation from the family setting, which brings a new quality of openness; how many adolescents and, even more, young adults, manage to remain open for the new; in touch with the new human being who wants to come to birth in every one of us? It is no coincidence that the sacramental biography of the human being which starts with baptism after birth and ends with the Last Anointing before death has as its middle point the Confirmation, long before the middle of an average human life. Much is decided in these years which determines the course of the rest of the person's life.

Because Christian initiation has become part of human biography, it is easy to see only that aspect of the sacraments which is generally human. If only this part is seen, they become mere developmental aids for growing up. The seriousness of the decision to enter the community of Jesus Christ and the deep experiences that Saint Paul describes, remind us that there is quite another aspect. Baptism and Confirmation are preparation and practice for membership in the community that gathers at the altar of offering, the community of those who have 'put off the body of flesh,' who were 'buried with him in Baptism' and 'raised with him through faith in the working of God, who raised him from the dead.' Creating a vessel in which the substance of this community can be formed is a demanding task.

Membership

The fact that neither baptized babies nor confirmed teenagers are counted as members of The Christian Community shows that the decision to become a full member of the Community is one that must be taken in complete freedom. For this reason The Christian Community has an open communion. However, this very openness makes the question of membership all the more important.

Church history has seen two attitudes to membership. Some churches have made firm boundaries which make very obvious whether one is inside or outside the church. Clear demands distinguish those within from the world outside. This has the virtue of clarity but the problem of exclusiveness. Then there is another type of church community, where the boundaries are blurred; all are welcome, but it remains unclear what being part of the church really means. This is a generous and inclusive gesture, but it is more difficult to know who is really responsible for the church.

The Act of Consecration of Man is a process of becoming a member of Christ's body. To join in the work of the community, uniting oneself with the stream of offering that flows from the world to the altar, and receiving the grace that streams towards one — this means to be membered into the body of Christ. This process of becoming members of one body can be traced through every Act of Consecration of Man.

Nevertheless there is a counterpart to this dynamic process of becoming a member, when I acknowledge publicly that I belong to this community. This has the character of a confession in the positive sense of the word. It means that the strong experience that made me come again and again to the Act of Consecration, to feel a part of the offering, perhaps even to take communion, is translated into a steady, committed will.

Many people feel wary of committing themselves to any earthly institutions, and perhaps to a church in particular. Nevertheless we also know that there are steps we take in life that seem to restrict our freedom, but which are in fact the gate into a greater freedom and creativity. Our freedom to be part of the Community depends on the decision of some at least to commit themselves. If no one became a member of The Christian Community, ultimately it could not continue to exist.

The priests' circle acknowledges this when it comes to assessing where new congregations can be founded. Here it is most important that there are sufficient members, as they are the ones who have made known their will for the Community.

Taking leave of the earthly community

At the end of life, another sacramental act can help the human soul to pass from the community of earth back to that of spirit.

In the oil used in the Anointing an image lights up of what will happen at the end of all things. Oil lubricates, warms and softens. It also releases light. Its sacramental quality is revealed in the words spoken to consecrate it before it is used in two rituals in The Christian Community — Ordination and Anointing. They speak of its connection to the quality of love.

Ideally the Anointing will be prepared by a Sacramental Consultation, and a final communion. In the Consultation, one's life can be reviewed and any thoughts that have not yet been brought into flow can be offered up. It is often important for someone approaching death to experience release from earthly burdens — sometimes a particular meeting is important here, before they can let go. Now they are ready to be part of the great service of offering of the Son of Man within them.

In the final communion, the one approaching death can experience once again being part of the community that offers and receives on earth. The Anointing itself leads the departing soul to the start of the journey that will take it back into communion with the spiritual world — into the new unity.

Celebrating community of life

There is nothing arbitrary about the seven moments that are lifted into the sacramental sphere. It would be easy to think of other moments — leaving school, for example, or retirement, that could be so dignified. And this gives us a clue that the organism of the sacraments has not just come about as a response to human need. It is the revelation of something archetypal. For this reason the Sacrament of Marriage is more than just a blessing of a challenging realm of life. It is an icon and an anticipation of the marriage of heaven and earth, that is already happening and will happen ever more.

In this way, the Sacrament of Marriage rightly understood is as inclusive as any other. It does not deny the value of other forms of relationship — civil partnership, or homosexual union. It is an icon of overcoming separateness, and for this reason the partners to be joined need to belong to each side of the original division, in that one is a man and one is a woman. It is the fulfilment of the promise made after the division into the sexes: 'Therefore shall a man leave his father and his mother, and shall cleave unto his wife: and they shall be one flesh.'

The Sacrament of Marriage refers to the marriage itself throughout as 'community of life.' This quality — in Greek, *koinonia* — is the quality of the Holy Spirit, as we saw above. Marriage is the icon of the *koinonia* of the Holy Spirit. It shows us that every true human relationship in which community of life can be lived is a window on the community of life which is the Trinity.

As the prophetic foretaste of God's community with humanity, the Sacrament of Marriage contains two powerful icons which are symbols of unity. These are the rings and the two sticks that are bound together. The words spoken over the rings, which are said to 'round off the corners of life' and to 'enclose the web of being' show that the rings embody the oneness that underlies all the multiplicity of the world. We have seen that this oneness is on a journey to a new unity in community. The joining of opposites in marriage is a foretaste of the new unity that we are to achieve in community.

In a very different symbol, the binding of the sticks also shows the tendency to unity. Two separate sticks are taken and bound in the form of a Saint Andrew's cross. Whilst the knot symbolizes the joining of two destinies in this moment, the fact that they are not bound parallel to each other shows that the two life-paths are to continue developing. The spiritual world looks upon this joining 'of what was apart that it become one' as a foretaste of what is to come — the new community which does not extinguish individuals but raises them to a higher unity.

The Sacrament of Marriage ends with a blessing and a promise that what has happened here has a dimension that goes far beyond the destinies of the individuals marrying. This earthly celebration of *koinonia*, the community of life between human beings, which is at the same time the celebration of the community of life between God and his creation is ultimately celebrated for 'the good and happiness of all mankind.'

11. The Structuring of the Community

In New Testament times, the whole church was seen as an icon of the new community between God and human beings. The church was the new Israel, a kingdom of priests that performed the priestly service for the whole world. Gradually, this changed. The mystery of the altar came to be seen as so remote, so far beyond human worthiness, that a division started to be made between the clergy and the laity. This is the situation expressed by the iconostasis — the wall of icons that screens the altar area — in the Orthodox tradition. With all the emphasis on community which is a strength of Orthodox practice in other areas, here a tendency has been preserved that originated in the fourth century: a barrier is placed between the human and the spiritual worlds. Human consciousness cannot go beyond this barrier. So from the situation in which the church was seen as a living symbol of God to the world, the clergy and the ritual have become an icon of the spiritual world to the congregation.

With this there went hand in hand the change in the meaning of the word 'laity.' In the New Testament, *laos* means the temple-community. When this word was first used for the church, it meant the community as a whole. After the change in the fourth century, it came to mean those members of the church who were not ordained.

If this represents one tendency, the architecture of some reformed churches represents another. Here, there is no altar. A minister stands in the middle of the congregation at a table or a lectern. In the images of iconostasis and table, we see two dynamics that have been frozen in architectural form. The iconostasis embodies the dynamic that flows from the altar into the world with complete objectivity. No matter who is present, and what their contribution to the mass might be, the mystery will take place, and the gift of Christ's body and blood will be given. The preacher at the lectern amongst the congregation embodies the dynamic that flows from the human world towards the spiritual. What human beings can understand and take into themselves is the decisive factor.

These two great movements meet and merge in every celebration of the Act of Consecration of Man. The congregation comes from the world; priest and servers come from the vestry, showing that the service has another origin. If we follow the course of the Act of Consecration with our eyes open even for what seems commonplace, we notice that the position of the priest is dynamic. He or she normally stands facing forward as the first amongst equals, as expressed in the opening words: 'Let us worthily fulfil ...' The priest represents the congregation to the divine world, as an icon of what human community can become. Seven times the priest turns to face the congregation, and there he or she appears as an icon of the divine world, an image that recalls the vision of the Son of Man in the Book of Revelation. The final words: 'thus it has been' express the objectivity of the event.

The Sacrament of Ordination makes this weaving between the two directions possible. In order to celebrate the mystery of the communion with God, who is himself a community of persons with differentiated functions, a differentiation is needed.

The Christian Community gathers laity and priests together for the Ordination. The priests, wearing vestments, sit at the front. After the great events of the Ordination have taken place, which confer the spiritual power to perform the sacraments, the celebrant speaks the promise that Christ will accompany the priest in what he or she does. The fragmented creation will be drawn into the new community with God through the work of the priest. Now the priests are sent out into their congregations. It becomes clear that they have not joined the ranks of priests in order to stay in the holy circle, but to work in the world. However, this movement of sending out, which would seem to dissolve the assembly of priests, is followed by a movement that almost seems to contradict it. The celebrant processes around the assembled priests, carrying the consecrated elements of bread and wine. For a moment the deeper reality of the priests' circle becomes apparent: it is a circle enclosed by the consecration. The sending out can only happen because the priests' circle has its spiritual substance; the priests' circle can only be enclosed because it sends the priests out.

The words that follow express the fact that the priests sent into their congregations can fulfil their priestly task through the recognition that the congregation bestows upon them. We start to see the Trinitarian dynamic of the church. It is one substance — one body of Christ. Within it we can distinguish the priests' circle and the laity, connected by their relationship to each other. Who here is the lover, and who the beloved? When thinking in Trinitarian terms, it is better not to assign roles in a static way. But it is clear that the current of communication — of connection and of recognition — is the Holy Spirit.

Community and congregation

There is a question which particularly concerns students of Rudolf Steiner who are also involved with The Christian Community, which is whether there is a fundamental difference between the kind of community that emerges around ritual practice, and that which comes about when human beings strive together without such forms. When we place these two forms of community life next to each other to compare them, as Rudolf Steiner did after the foundation of The Christian Community, we see two complementary gestures.[21] The ritual 'brings the supersensible down into the physical world with its words and actions.' The work of the anthroposophical group without ritual forms 'raises the thoughts and feelings of the assembled individuals into the supersensible.' However, when we look at either movement by itself, we find both dynamics contained within it. In the case of the Act of Consecration, they are contained in the Offertory and Communion respectively.

Sacramental working does not substitute for or overturn what striving human beings can and shall do. Each of the sacraments can be found in everyday life. An example of this is the progress that has been in the realm of conversation in recent decades. The Sacramental Consultation can bring about a unique intensity in the encounter between priest and member. However, one would have to be blind or arrogant to dismiss all the work that has been done on conversation, and the methods that have been developed to allow reflection to take place without judgment. Alongside much that is questionable precisely because it lacks the spiritual dimension, we see as well the seeds of a culture in which every conversation is sacramental. Another example of the progress towards a sacramental attitude that extends far beyond the walls of a church is the work of some modern artists, such as van Gogh, whose attitude to the earth was a forerunner of the devotion to the earth that will see in every part of it the body of Christ.

From this point of view, what we do as a religious community is part of the great work, the great tendency towards a truly human way of living that is striving to unfold in our time. Part of our task of witness is to find this tendency, to celebrate and strengthen it. The Russian Orthodox theologian Alexander Schmemann described this with great clarity:

> The only real fall of man is his noneucharistic life in a noneucharistic world. ... Man was to be the priest of a Eucharist, offering the world to God, and in this offering he was to receive the gift of life. ... When we see the world as an end in itself, everything becomes itself a value and consequently loses all value, because only in God is found the meaning (value) of everything, and the world is meaningful only when it is the 'sacrament' of God's presence.
> (Schmemann 1967, pp.17–18)

Epilogue: The Future Hope

In the beginning was unity. Everything was infolded, potential. Then Godself overflowed in self-giving love and potential became reality. The great process of development began, with all its variety, its strayings, its sufferings and its glories.

We cannot begin to imagine the vastness of the number of atoms, molecules and organisms that have evolved; the richness and variety of all the feelings and thoughts of human beings and the joys and sorrows of their destinies on earth; the ranks of angelic beings and their work.

We find ourselves in this world of unimaginable richness, and yet we know what it means when we read in the Bible that this is a world that has lost its connection with its original unity with God. It is easy to doubt whether we have moved on from the time of Babel, the culture inspired by fear of the loss of connection to the spirit, whose pride and hubris brought about the splintering of humanity, breeding fear and suspicion among human beings. But then we hear of examples of humanity that surpass all our expectations, and we realize that we live in a world which is still open, where it is not yet decided which tendency will prevail.

The final book of the Bible, the Revelation to St John, predicts a final fulfilment when heaven and earth will be one again. A marriage takes place between heaven and earth, and creation has become a bride. The union of bride and groom does not undo the division into the sexes. It is a higher union, in which the qualities of each of these opposites remain, complementing and enhancing each other. When the prodigal son returns, the father, who seemed to have been impoverished by his going, in fact proves to have been enriched, for the waste and suffering caused by the son's reckless journey have made the son into a communion-partner, one who can share in the meal that celebrates new life from death. In the marriage between heaven and earth the journey proves to have been valuable — the world has evolved, human beings have progressed, and God has been enriched.

Does anything remain outside the stream of development, which cannot be integrated into the new union? Origen was condemned for teaching the restoration of all things, echoing Paul:

> The last enemy to be destroyed is death. For he 'has put
> everything under his feet.' … When he has done this,
> then the Son himself will be made subject to him who
> put everything under him, so that God may be all in all.
> (1 Corinthians 15:26, 28 NIV)

We have seen how the idea of reincarnation gives us a liberating perspective on our lives. We can often grasp intuitively what we need to do to advance on our path; often however we have to acknowledge that we can hardly imagine making this progress in this one earthly life. When the Act of Consecration of Man speaks of future 'cycles of time,' we can imagine that the progress of all beings, even those who fall out of the stream of development in one particular cycle, has other cycles to be fulfilled in. Will all be integrated in the stream again? This question does not demand our intellectual speculation but our realization that our own struggles are part of the cosmic struggle to decide whether the good will be the overwhelming tendency.

Our challenge and our calling is to find our true vocation in community — community with each other, with creation, and with God. There is nothing narrow or dogmatic in this community. It longs to embrace everyone and everything and to draw it into the great dynamic of the journey to the higher unity. Only when the new community includes everything and everyone will the journey prove to have enriched God, as the father was enriched by the return of his son in the parable. We are called to live community as a witness to the world, as a foretaste, a prophetic icon of the new unity which is the deepest longing of everything that is.

All the broken and dislocated pieces of the universe —
people and things, animals and atoms — get properly
fixed and fit together in vibrant harmonies, all because of
his death, his blood that poured down from the cross.
(Colossians 1:18, *The Message*)

Notes

1. See Steiner's *Occult Science* for a systematic description of this.
2. See, for example, Steiner's *Building Stones for an Understanding of the Mystery of Golgotha.*
3. See John Taylor, *The Go-Between God.*
4. See, for example, the work of Metropolitan Vassily Drozdov Filaret (1782–1867) cited in Gorodetzky 1938.
5. See Buber 1991, pp. x–xi.
6. For a further discussion of this very technical issue, see Debus 2000, p. 117.
7. See Botterweck and Ringgren (eds.), pp. 75–87.
8. For a detailed and insightful discussion of this phenomenon, see *Affluenza* by Oliver James.
9. The Definition of Chalcedon is quoted here from Stevenson 1993, pp. 352f.
10. See Steiner's lecture of October 5, 1911, in *From Jesus to Christ.*
11. For an extended and beautiful exposition of the working of the Spirit in the process of evolution, see Taylor 1972.
12. Compare the Council of Constantinople IV of the year 870: '"Spirit" signifies that from creation man is ordered to a supernatural end and that his soul can gratuitously be raised beyond all it deserves to communion with God.' DS 657 quoted in *Catechism of the Catholic Church,* p. 83.
13. *Timaeus,* 36
14. Origen, *On First Principles,* II 6:6.
15. See, for instance, Sparrow 1995.
16. The Council of Trent was the Nineteenth Ecumenical Council of the Roman Catholic Church. It convened in Trent between December 13, 1545, and December 4, 1563, in twenty-five sessions for three periods.
17. See Frieling 1977, and Rittelmeyer 1988.
18. See also Capel and Ravetz, 1999.
19. Compare Colossians 3:3.
20. See the booklet by Hans-Werner Schroeder, *The Gospel Readings in the Course of the Year.*
21. See, for example, Steiner 1974, Lecture 9, p. 156.

Sources and References

Bible quotations are from the Revised Standard Version (RSV) unless otherwise indicated. Other versions used and acknowledged are:
The Message — the Bible in Contemporary Language, translated by Eugene H. Peterson, NavPress, Colorado Springs, 2003.
New International Version (NIV), Hodder & Stoughton Ltd, London, 1992.

Augustine (1983) *The Confessions of Saint Augustine*, Hodder and Stoughton, London.
Beck, Martha (1999) *Expecting Adam — a True Story of Birth, Rebirth, and Everyday Magic*, Berkley Trade, New York.
Botterweck and Ringgren (eds.) (1977) *Theological Dictionary of the Old Testament*, Vol. 1, Eerdmans, Grand Rapids.
Buber, Martin (1991) *Tales of the Hasidim: Book One: The Early Masters* and *Book Two: The Later Masters*, Schocken Books, New York.
Catechism of the Catholic Church (1994) Geoffrey Chapman, London.
Campbell, Alistair (1986) *Rediscovering Pastoral Care*, DLT, London.
Capel, Evelyn and Tom Ravetz (1999) *Seven Sacraments in The Christian Community*, Floris Books, Edinburgh.
Celan, Paul (1980) *Collected Poems — a Bilingual Edition*, Persea Books, New York.
Chidester, David (2000) *Christianity — A Global History*, Penguin Books, London.
Cyril of Jerusalem (1893) *Mystagogical Catechism*, in *A Select Library of the Nicene and Post-Nicene Fathers of the Christian Church* (Second Series) Vol. II, Book 7, Christian Literature Publishing Co., New York.
Debus, Michael (2000) *Maria-Sophia — Das Element des Weiblichen im Werden der Menschheit*, Verlag Freies Geistesleben, Stuttgart.
Dostoevsky, Fyodor (2002) *The Brothers Karamazov*, Plain Label Books.
Eliot, T.S. (1974) *Collected Poems 1909–1962*, Faber and Faber, London.
Filaret, Vassily (1938) *Works, Words and Sermons*, Moscow, 1814. Cited in Gorodetzky 1938.
Frieling, Rudolf (1977) *Christianity and Reincarnation*, Floris Books, Edinburgh.
Gorodetzky, Nadejda (1938) *The Humiliated Christ in Modern Russian Thought*, SPCK, London.

Harvey, Nicholas Peter (1991) *The Morals of Jesus,* DLT, London.
Hick, John (2004), 'Christ in a Universe of Faith,' from
    www.qug.org.uk/HICK6.DOC
Hopkins, Gerard Manley (1970) *The Poems of Gerard Manley Hopkins,* ed.
    Gardner *et al,* OUP, Oxford.
James, Oliver (2007) *Affluenza,* Vermillion, London.
Lewis, C.S. (1985) *The Voyage of the Dawn Treader,* Fontana Lions, London.
Lusseyran, Jacques (1985) *And there was Light,* Floris Books, Edinburgh.
Maybaum, Ignaz (1965) *The Face of God after Auschwitz,* Polak & Van
    Gennep Ltd, Amsterdam.
Mascaró, Juan (1993) *The Bhagavad Gita,* SCM Press Ltd, London.
Moltmann, Jürgen (2002) *Theology of Hope,* SCM Press, London.
Origen, *On First Principles,* from
    http://www.ccel.org/ccel/schaff/anf04.vi.v.i.html.
Patrick, *Confession of Saint Patrick,* from
    http://www.ccel.org/ccel/patrick/confession.txt.
Rittelmeyer, Friedrich (1988) *Reincarnation,* Floris Books, Edinburgh.
Schleiermacher, Friedrich (1999) *The Christian Faith,* T. & T. Clark,
    Edinburgh.
Schroeder, Hans-Werner (2008) *The Gospel Readings in the Course of the
    Year,* Floris Books, Edinburgh.
Schmemann, Alexander (1967) *For the Life of the World,* St Vladimir's
    Seminary Press, Crestwood, NY.
Sparrow, G. Scott (1995) *I am with You Always — True Stories of Encounters
    with Jesus,* Pan Books, London.
Steiner, Rudolf (1969) *Knowledge of the Higher Worlds — How is it
    Achieved?,* Rudolf Steiner Press, UK.
—, (1972) *Building Stones for an Understanding of the Mystery of Golgotha,*
    Rudolf Steiner Press, UK.
—, (1974) *Awakening to Community,* Anthroposophic Press, Hudson, NY.
—, (2005A) *From Jesus to Christ,* Rudolf Steiner Press, UK.
—, (2005B), *Occult Science,* Rudolf Steiner Press, UK.
Stevenson, J. (revised W.H.C. Frend) (1993) *Creeds, Councils and Contro-
    versies — Documents Illustrating the History of the Church,* AD 337–461,
    SPCK, London.
Taylor, John (1972) *The Go-Between God,* SPCK, London.
Wiesel, Elie (2006) *Night, Penguin,* London.

Film

The Wave (2008). Director: Dennis Gansel.

Index